THE ALICE MUNRO PAPERS
FIRST ACCESSION

ERRATA

Page xiv. Replace the last sentence in the 3rd paragraph with the following:

''Baptizing'' was written next, followed by the two opening stories and, after much agonizing, the epilogue (Struthers interview).

THE ALICE MUNRO PAPERS
FIRST ACCESSION:
An Inventory of the Archive
at
THE UNIVERSITY OF CALGARY LIBRARIES

COMPILERS
Jean M. Moore
Jean F. Tener

EDITORS
Apollonia Steele
Jean F. Tener

BIOCRITICAL ESSAY
Thomas E. Tausky

THE UNIVERSITY OF CALGARY PRESS

1986

© 1986 The University of Calgary. All rights reserved

ISBN 0-919813-44-5
ISSN 0831-4497

The University of Calgary Press
2500 University Drive N.W.
Calgary, Alberta, Canada T2N 1N4

Canadian Cataloguing in Publication Data

University of Calgary. Libraries. Special
  Collections Division.
    The Alice Munro papers, first accession
    (Canadian archival inventory series,
    ISSN 0831-4497 ; no. 7)
    ISBN 0-919813-44-5

    1. Munro, Alice, 1931-   -Archives -
Catalogs. 2. University of Calgary.
Libraries. Special Collections Division -
Catalogs. 3. Archives - Alberta - Calgary -
Catalogs. I. Moore, Jean M., 1935-
II. Tener, Jean, 1931-   III. Steele,
Apollonia. IV. Title. V. Series.
PS8576.U56Z991 1986   016.813'54   C86-091385-6
Z8605.62.U54 1986

Canadian Archival Inventory Series: Literary Papers. No. 7

Series editor: Charles R. Steele

Printed in Canada

Series Introduction

The establishment of the Canadian Studies — Research Tools Program by the Social Sciences and Humanities Research Council of Canada has formally acknowledged the frequently lamented absence from the field of Canadian Studies of such basic documents of research as indexes, inventories and bibliographies. This relative absence has frustrated the extensive and/or efficient use by scholars of the potentially rich materials presently held in and being acquired by Canadian research institutions. Consequently much research that could be done, and that should be done, is not being done. It is the aim of the Canadian Archival Inventories Series at the University of Calgary to contribute to the amelioration of this situation by providing basic research documentation which will, we hope, stimulate scholars to undertake the kinds of elementary investigation that have long been needed in Canadian Studies.

Charles R. Steele

Acknowledgements

The preparation of this inventory has been made possible by the generous support of the Social Sciences and Humanities Research Council of Canada under its Strategic Grants — Research Tools Program.

The project members are grateful to Mrs. Carol Hansen, Arts and Humanities Area Library, who has entered the data and produced the hard copy text.

Many thanks are also given to Shirley Onn for her patient and careful copy editing.

Table of Contents

37.16.37
[1960s]

Morning

swamp

~ Water River ~ × Founder C.N. R~

Mason

Park × Peace

Crements × Peace

wat. H Street
X PO

Cedar

Map of Jubilee
in notebook MsC 37.16.37

Biocritical Essay
by
Thomas E. Tausky

Widely regarded as Canada's best writer of short stories, Alice
Munro has consistently produced work in which precise social observation
and penetrating psychological insight are complemented by an unerring
instinct for exactly the right form of expression.

Alice Laidlaw was born in Wingham, a small Huron County town,
in 1931. Her father's family had lived in Western Ontario for several
generations, whereas her mother's family had settled in the Ottawa
Valley. In the Depression, Robert Laidlaw found little success as a
breeder of silver foxes. His wife, previously a school teacher, at one
time sold the furs at a Muskoka resort to help the family survive. Alice
Munro has described this episode, which reveals her father's stoicism and
her mother's determination, in a recently published memoir, "Working for
a Living".

In several forthright and revealing interviews, Munro has
commented on both her outer circumstances and her inner life during the
period of her childhood. The Laidlaw house was a little distance from the
town (as in the "Flats Road" section of Lives of Girls and Women); Alice
attended a primary school much like the rough school portrayed in the
"Privilege" story of Who Do You Think You Are?. "Life was fairly
dangerous", Munro has told Alan Twigg. She continued:

> We lived outside the whole social structure because we
> didn't live in the town and we didn't live in the
> country. We lived in this kind of little ghetto where
> all the bootleggers and prostitutes and hangers-on
> lived. Those were the people I knew. It was a
> community of outcasts. I had that feeling about
> myself.

Depressing as this situation sounds, Munro was undismayed: "I thought
my life was interesting. There was always a great sense of adventure".

Munro found herself to be an outsider in spirit as well as social
position. She grew up in a "very traditional community" (Graeme Gibson
interview), a society in which "it's necessary...always to think practically
...I always realized that I had a different view of the world, and one
that would bring me into great trouble and ridicule if it were exposed".
For her own protection, therefore, "I always operated in disguises"
(Gibson), a strategy many of her fictional characters were to adopt.

Adolescence for Munro was a time of divided values and

loyalties. She told the present writer:

> As a child, I always felt separate, but pretty happy to be so. Then in high school, suddenly with puberty and everybody getting down to business – girls especially getting down to what their role would be – I began to feel terribly out of things and in a way superficially unhappy about that because I wanted to be an ordinary girl. I wanted to be very attractive to boys, and I wanted to go out, and I wanted to get married, and get a diamond: those things, more or less as signs of being a fully OK kind of woman. The plan to write got crystallized about puberty too, and I was actually doing it all the time. And I was quite happy in that world. (Interview, July 20, 1984; next five quotations from an interview are from this source.)

Munro began writing down her stories at the age of twelve, beginning with imitative adventure stories. She also indulged in daydreams picturing herself in heroic roles (as the protagonist does in the story "Boys and Girls"), but she now feels that it was the impulse to imitate that defined the potential writer: "Trying to make a story like 'The Little Mermaid' [by Hans Christian Andersen] and then later on trying to make a story like Wuthering Heights: those were not daydream stories – there was some apprehension there of what fiction is". The Bronte imitation, a bleak work entitled Charlotte Muir for which much was imagined but only the death scenes were written down, now seems to Munro to have allegorical significance: "I can see what was going on. I can see that those were the twin choices of my life, which were marriage and motherhood, or the black life of the artist".

Munro's private dedication to her writing was a great source of confidence in her teenage years. She recalls:

> I felt able to cope with everything. I really felt so buoyed up, so excited, by this writing thing that I had latched on to. It gave me in those years the most enormous happiness. I was quite stunned by what I was able to do, at fifteen or sixteen. It's just that way of being able to translate a kind of rapture that I think everybody feels – the thing is to find a way of expressing it. And I really felt able to do that then.

Munro won a scholarship to attend the University of Western Ontario. "The Dimensions of a Shadow", her first published story, appeared in Folio, the student literary magazine, when Munro was an eighteen-year-old freshman. The magazine's notes on "The Contributors" describe Alice Laidlaw as follows: "Overly modest about her talents, but hopes to write the Great Canadian Novel someday". Folio published two other stories, "Story for Sunday" and "The Widower", in subsequent issues.

Alice Laidlaw left Western after only two years. Her scholarship was for a two-year period, and she simply had no more money. Shortly afterwards, she married James Munro, and the couple settled in Vancouver. Two children, Sheila (b. 1953) and Jenny (b. 1957), were born early in the marriage; a third daughter, Andrea, was born in 1966. For several years, James Munro worked as an Eaton's executive in Vancouver. With his wife's assistance, he subsequently opened a bookshop in Victoria.

Living in a Vancouver suburb, Alice Munro lost the faith in her artistic powers she had felt as an adolescent:

> The big period of the failure of confidence all came in
> my twenties, not in my adolescence at all. I began,
> as every artist does, to get a much more realistic
> notion of what those powers were, and that combined
> with a life in which there was not too much opportu-
> nity to work, and not too much recognition - well,
> really no recognition, except I always mention that my
> husband recognized it because without that I couldn't
> have survived.

The stimulus an interesting environment could provide was no longer available: "It was much more enclosed in the suburbs than Wingham was. It was much more boring. I have never even been able to do much with it fictionally because I hated it so much".

All these factors slowed Munro's output in the Fifties and Sixties. Nevertheless, she wrote several stories which were accepted by Robert Weaver for broadcast by the CBC, and her stories appeared in such journals as The Canadian Forum, Tamarack Review, Queen's Quarterly, The Montrealer, and, in a brief fling of commercial success, Chatelaine. Fifteen stories were collected in Dance of the Happy Shades (1968), a volume assembled with the encouragement of Earle Topping and Audrey Coffin of the Ryerson Press. The book won the Governor General's Award, but had not sold out its first printing of 2,500 copies by 1972 (John Metcalf interview).

In interviews with Metcalf and J. R. (Tim) Struthers, Munro has given a chronology of the stories included in Dance of the Happy Shades, and has also provided a commentary on their place in the evolution of her work. She regards the stories written from 1953 to 1959 ("The Time of Death" and "Day of the Butterfly" are the two earliest, followed by "An Ounce of Cure", "Thanks for the Ride", "Sunday Afternoon", "The Shining Houses" and "A Trip to the Coast") as essentially "exercise stories...the work of a beginning writer" (Metcalf interview). In the Summer of 1959, Munro wrote "The Peace of Utrecht", which she sees as a major turning-point in her career: "It was the first story I absolutely had to write and wasn't writing to see if I could write that kind of a story" (Struthers interview). In this story, Munro dealt with a very personal subject, her own mother's illness (Mrs. Laidlaw had contracted Parkinson's Disease when her daughter was twelve). Munro came to this material hesitantly and involuntarily rather than through straightforward choice. She now feels, however, that the self-understanding she thereby acquired brought an artistic breakthrough:

> That [the writing of "The Peace of Utrecht"] came
> out of my mother's death. Until my mother died,
> though the relationship with her was a very painful,
> deep one, I wasn't able to look at it or think about
> it....It's as if up to a certain point I was much more
> an artist than a person. I was essentially fairly tight
> emotionally. (Tausky interview)

Most of the Dance of the Happy Shades stories written after "The Peace of Utrecht" have autobiographical elements. "The Office" is based directly on an actual incident. "Boys and Girls" recalls the modest expectations ("She's only a girl") reserved for girls in Huron County. "Red Dress-1946" reflects the competing temptations of social acceptance and independent womanhood. "Walker Brothers Cowboy" fictionalizes the social and economic decline of the Laidlaw family, and also draws on a specific occurrence:

> When I was a much younger child, my father took me
> for some reason I've forgotten to that woman's house,
> and she taught me how to dance. There was some-
> thing about the revelation of this whole Catholic style
> of life that seemed much freer and jollier and poorer
> - if you can imagine poorer than ours!"
> (Tausky interview)

Though none of Munro's stories are without interest, the line she draws at "The Peace of Utrecht" does seem to divide well crafted but slight stories from those which demanded greater resources of feeling and understanding. In three stories especially - "Images", "Walker Brothers Cowboy" and "The Peace of Utrecht" - Munro attains a richness of suggestion that has continued to characterize her work. "The Peace of

Utrecht", one of Munro's best stories of family bonds and bondage, had as its starting point the author's own experience of being offered her mother's clothes by her aunt and grandmother. The narrator and her sister both have a burden of guilt: the narrator has left her sister to shoulder the responsibility of caring for their chronically ill mother; Maddy has ultimately found it necessary to put her mother in a nursing home. The narrator states flatly at the beginning of the story that she and her sister "at heart reject each other", yet as the story unfolds, the sisters' emotional ties seem to matter as much as their opposed choices in life. Moreover, the narrator is linked to her sister, her mother and even her aunt, in that each, with greater or lesser success, has "tried to run".

"Images" and "Walker Brothers Cowboy" have in common that they both deal with the "bewilderment" that is the young imagination's response to dark experiences. The narrator in both stories pledges to share her father's secret. In "Images", the narrator feels herself to be ambivalently "dazed and powerful with secrets"; in "Walker Brothers Cowboy", the spell she is under disconcerts and also threatens the loss of control: the "enchantment" can change "into something you will never know". In each case, the allusion to fairy stories, while appropriate to the narrator's situation, at the same time suggests the author's continuing interest in the expression of the imagination through romance.

In "Images", a sombre romance atmosphere prevails throughout the dramatization of an encounter with a paranoid recluse. "Walker Brothers Cowboy" is an extremely poignant story within the realm of mundane experience. As in much of Munro's work, the narrator's inner drama complements the spiritual turmoil she observes. The narrator is the victim of time in two contexts: she faces her own insignificance in geological time at the beginning of the story, and in the story's conclusion she grapples with the mystery of her father's love affair before her birth. Meanwhile, her father and his former girl friend have been robbed by the years of the possibility that their relationship might be renewed:

"We've taken a lot of your time now".

"Time", says Nora bitterly. "Will you come by ever again"?

Together with its haunting psychological veracity, "Walker Brothers Cowboy" has in abundance that other striking feature of Munro's fiction, her extraordinarily vivid re-creation of physical reality. Many paragraphs from the story could be chosen to illustrate Munro's ability to evoke not only a place (a Lake Huron town like Goderich), but also a sense of period (the Depression). In part, this power is derived from a gift of nature. Munro has told Kem Murch: "I remember all experience very vividly....Last year I saw a black-and-white photo of my high school class that was taken in grade 10, and I did remember the colour of everyone's clothes". Of equal importance, however, is a strong emotional attachment to the tangible properties of reality. She has told Graeme Gibson that this attitude comes close to a kind of religious feeling about the world; speaking to Geoff Hancock a decade later, she remarked that:

> Even totally commonplace things...are just sort of
> endlessly interesting in their physical reality. I find
> them that way. That they seem to mean something
> way beyond themselves.

The work of other writers has probably been most important to Munro when it has provided an external sanction for her own inclination to present reality concretely, minutely, but also through the filter of a very individual, fully realized sensibility. It is in following this artistic path, rather than in making explicit borrowings, that Munro has gained from the example of such Southern writers as James Agee, Eudora Welty and Reynolds Price.

Yet another factor contributing to the success of Munro's stories is the immense care she lavishes upon their composition. The University of Calgary papers provide a privileged opportunity to observe a superb intuitive imagination at work. Often completely separate drafts are created for the sake of seemingly minor, but in reality crucial, adjustments of nuances in the choice of word or incident.

The Calgary papers also allow their reader to follow the complicated artistic challenges and decisions Munro took upon herself in writing her second book, Lives of Girls and Women (1971). This work, composed over a relatively short period of time – about a year – nevertheless involved writing crises in its early and concluding phases. Munro began the book with the intention of producing a conventional novel, but came to realize that the medium of separate but inter-linked stories was more suited to her talent. The abandoned novel, in re-written form, became the middle section of the book, from "Princess Ida" through to the story "Lives of Girls and Women". The two opening stories were written next, followed by "Baptizing", and, after much agonizing, the epilogue (Struthers interview).

Munro had been thinking about Lives of Girls and Women for some years before she turned her full attention to the book. One can find several links with the mature stories of Dance of the Happy Shades. Del Jordan is not the first Munro protagonist to have to struggle with poverty and isolation. Like the Jordan girl of "Walker Brothers Cowboy", Del has an ambitious, dissatisfied mother, and a gentle, detached father; like the narrator of "The Peace of Utrecht", she has prudent aunts; like the narrator of "Red Dress-1946" she faces a choice between conventional and unconventional directions for her life; like the protagonist of "Images" she has to confront madness and death.

Del can, nevertheless, be distinguished from her predecessors (and indeed, from many of her successors) in the Munro canon by virtue of her ability to act firmly, confidently and constructively in order to shape her own future. She makes up her mind about the various members of her family, and doles out proportionate quantities of love and trust; she pursues an independent course in finding her way into and out of a religious crisis; she overcomes the temptation of sexual submission. Right from the opening pages, there are grim events in Lives of Girls and Women, but the central character's freedom to experiment and choose for herself gives the book a light-hearted spirit not always found in Munro's work. The self-assurance Del exhibits derives from the confidence Munro herself felt in adolescence: the book "probably accurately reflects my own emotional and artistic life as a teenager" (Tausky interview).

The title is a meaningful indication of the book's nature. Male figures are given roles of some prominence, but only as supporting actors in the drama of Del's life. The characters who linger in the memory as powerfully imagined creations are all women: Del herself, her mother, her mother's boarder Fern, her aunts. The aunts are evoked with special brilliance, both as individuals and as representatives of country values.

Munro presents with wry affection the aunts' world of "work and gaiety, comfort and order, intricate formality". For a person of Del's determined and adventurous temperament, however, the charms of the aunts fade when the danger of their prideful humility is grasped. Del's straightforward escape from her aunts' principles finds no counterpart in her tangled, ambivalent feelings about her mother. If Aunt Elspeth and Auntie Grace are marvellous comic inventions, Del's mother is a penetrating study in a more serious style. As Del herself comes to realize, she is in perpetual conflict with her mother because she is so much like her. Del's condescending judgment of her mother is always made available to the reader, but is not always an accurate guide. Addie's righteous secularism needs to be evaluated with sympathy in the light of the fanatical piety embraced by her own mother; her naive, and in its own way, touching, trust in knowledge is to be understood in relation to the virulent anti-intellectualism of her surroundings. On the other hand, it is unwise to swallow whole, as some critics have done, Addie's now famous words, "There is a change coming I think in the lives of girls and women". The passage is an apt expression of Addie's meliorist views, rather than the sudden intrusion of a feminist lecture.

Lives of Girls and Women could easily have ended with Del's rejection of Garnet French's claim upon her. Indeed, it almost did: Munro at one point was so unhappy with her efforts to write the "Epilogue" section that she told her publisher to leave it out of the book. Munro's painstaking efforts to get the epilogue right can be observed in the numerous drafts preserved in the Calgary papers. What finally emerged from this travail was a major addition to the novel that also substantially altered its character. Munro has underlined its significance in her interview with Struthers:

> Up until now this was not the story of the artist as a young girl. It was just the story of a young girl. And this introduced a whole new element, which I felt hadn't been sufficiently prepared for. And yet, I found eventually that the book didn't mean anything to me without it.

To some readers, Del's resolve to abjure romance fantasies and to embrace the facts of Jubilee life adds up to an endorsement of realism. Not so, Munro states:

> People have taken this to mean more of a siding with realistic writing than I would take it to mean. I'm not making judgments there....It's not a direct plumping in favour of a certain kind of writing because that dark stuff keeps coming back to me even now. You see, it hasn't gone. (Tausky interview)

The "dark stuff" of Gothic fiction is represented in the epilogue by the story of the photographer. Munro had worked on versions of this tale years before she wrote Lives of Girls and Women. Though Del adopts an attitude of self-mockery towards this "black fable", it does indeed contain the "powerful" implications she ironically ascribes to it. The photographer who takes "unusual, even frightening" pictures and thereby intimidates the community, is the naive writer's allegorical vision of the artist's dark power. The story also contains the implication that art needs to go beyond the documentary level to achieve its effect.

Del turns for inspiration to the more homely materials of her existence: Bobby Sherriff's curiously matter-of-fact conversation, lists of businesses and of street-names. Coupled with the novelist's imagination, this information is to provide the foundation of Del's new literary art. The evocative phrase "deep caves paved with kitchen linoleum" has been taken, with some justice, to be an appropriate description of Munro's own method.

Yet Del's new-found technique is not presented without

reservations and qualifications. "Damage had been done" to Del's Gothic novel, but she has found its replacement only in anticipation. The task before her is daunting, for "the hope of accuracy...is crazy, heart-breaking" and lists will not suffice. A telling comparison is invoked in Del's suggestion that she is "voracious and misguided as Uncle Craig out at Jenkin's Bend, writing his history". Del will not, presumably, echo the tedious literalism of Uncle Craig's narrative, but the mention of his name reminds us that there are literary dangers in adherence to fact, just as there are risks in neglecting fact. In coming to understand the complex blend of madness and the mundane to be found in Bobby Sherriff's character, Del has deepened her understanding of the mysteriousness of life; in repudiating dramatic inventiveness, she has renounced a valuable means of portraying that dimension of life (Del has voluntarily denied herself the principal means Munro used to deal with this kind of subject in "Images"). Munro's labours in multiplying drafts can be seen as an effort to strike a viable balance between the sense of profit and of loss involved in Del's adoption of her new literary strategy. The third-to-last paragraph is not contained in any of the early drafts – Munro has said that it was only "when that [paragraph] came to me" that she knew "I could leave it [the epilogue] in" (Tausky interview). Bobby Sherriff's enigmatic gesture is a "special thing" which gives Del both pleasure and the insight of an epiphany; on the other hand, it is only "a letter, or a whole word" in "an alphabet I did not know". The incident therefore captures in miniature the mixture of new knowledge and open-ended challenges that is also to be found in the section as a whole.

Something I've Been Meaning to Tell You (1974), Munro's second collection of unrelated stories, is the Janus volume in her development as a writer. Stories like "Winter Wind" or "The Found Boat" might have been at home in Dance of the Happy Shades: the family tensions of the one story and the condescension towards girls of the other, both within the Huron County setting, constitute familiar material. "Executioners", with its grisly ending, is a reversion to an even earlier Gothic phase. But stories such as "Walking on Water" and "Forgiveness in Families" are studies in the hippie and cult movements of the time, and "Marrakesh" and "The Spanish Lady" almost seem like anticipations of The Moons of Jupiter in their dramatizations of a new protagonist, the sophisticated, intellectually inclined woman suffering through fragile relationships. Many of the stories seem designed to discard polished, but also contrived, effects in favour of an acceptance of stylistic and narrative fragmentation as a mirror of fragmented lives.

Among the most ambitious and accomplished stories in the volume are "Memorial", "Material" and "The Ottawa Valley". "Memorial" and "Material" are built upon a characteristic Munro situation, the tensions inherent in the linkage of two people with opposite temperaments. "Memorial", like "The Peace of Utrecht", is a story of sisters, but in the more recent story the narrative is told from the perspective of the more contemplative, less assertive sister. Eileen may not grasp the technique of garbage re-cycling, but June's "built, planned, lived deliberately, filled life" is mocked by the events of the story - the accidental death of June's son and the impulsive seduction of Eileen by June's husband. With its sardonic treatment of June's hollow "Memorial Party" and her attempt to "live by values", "Memorial" is in part a satiric commentary on the quest for faith in a post-religious world, a theme also raised in "Walking on Water".

The religion of art is subjected to a heretic's exegesis in "Material", one of Munro's most dazzling feats in balancing poignancy and comedy. The narrator's re-examination of her previous life as a matrimonial servant of the artist is precipitated when she discovers her ex-husband's short story about a person who was part of their shared past. Dotty, the "harlot-in-residence" who takes in customers in a basement apartment below Hugo and the narrator, is a pathetic figure worthy of compassion to the narrator, merely "material" to the writer. The "special, unsparing, unsentimental love" Hugh eventually bestows upon Dotty in his story is "not enough", his ex-wife ultimately decides, after initial admiration for his achievement. "Material" cleverly incorporates several levels: it is a persuasive study in individual psychology, with the narrator's judgment of Hugo (and, by implication, her own self-esteem) in doubt until the end; it raises the wider question of the validity of distinctions based on gender (the narrator becomes convinced that Hugo and her very different present husband "both have authority" and she does not); it is a story, and a subtle one, about the act of writing itself. The narrator is in the unusual position of documenting a personality who, thanks to her ex-husband, has already "passed into Art". The story, therefore, resembles the conclusion to Lives of Girls and Women in using alternative methods of representation as a means of arousing the reader's active interest in the process whereby reality is made into fiction.

The potential in art to falsify reality is raised as an issue yet again in the final paragraph of "The Ottawa Valley". Indeed, by the time this final story of the volume came to be written, Munro herself had grown so distrustful of ficitonalizing that she seriously contemplated giving up the writing of fiction altogether. Munro's own testimony is that the story is autobiographical; the protagonist's dilemma in having to choose between "making a proper story" of her mother's illness and wanting "to bring back all I could" may reflect the author's own quandary. The apparently episodic quality of the story gives it the air of a painfully sincere recollection, art giving the impression of avoiding the contamination of artifice.

In Who Do You Think You Are? (1978), Munro returned to the method of inter-locking stories she had adopted for Lives of Girls and Women. The books also have in common a complicated pre-publication history. In both the Struthers and the Hancock interview, Munro has given a detailed account of an earlier conception of Who Do You Think You Are?, according to which some of the stories eventually about Rose were narrated by another character named Janet. The book was to be half Janet stories and half Rose stories, a structure Munro felt "was just too fancy" (Hancock interview). Then, after the volume was in galleys, Munro quickly wrote "Simon's Luck" and the title story, and killed off Janet. Three Janet stories ("Connection", "The Stone in the Field" and "The Moons of Jupiter") eventually were included in The Moons of Jupiter.

Who Do You Think You Are? was written after Munro moved back to Western Ontario from British Columbia. Her marriage with James Munro had dissolved, and she married Gerald Fremlin, a fellow under-graduate when she was a student at Western. Munro has told Hancock that when she returned to Huron County "one of the things I noticed immediately was the class system". This perception soon found a fictional translation in Who Do You Think You Are?: Hanratty is a far more class-ridden community, as well as far more violent and menacing, than Jubilee.

Beaten by her father, hearing tales about vigilante justice, witnessing incest in the Entryway of the Boys' Toilet at school, Munro's new protagonist Rose has one educational challenge: "learning to survive". This is, indeed, the task she is engaged in throughout the book, as she moves from childhood by way of an unsuccessful marriage into a precarious middle age. Like the narrator of "Material", she feels that it is her individual destiny, and the fate of her sex, never to be "the free person, the one with that power".

Del Jordan did have much of that freedom, and Lives of Girls and Women consequently has an easily understood unity: in each successive story, Del tests her capacities in relation to some basic experience of life - religion, sex, authorship. Such a straightforward, confident assault upon reality is foreign to the world of Munro's more recent fiction. As she said to Hancock: "What I have is people going on ....There are just flashes of things we know and find out. I don't see life very much in terms of progress".

Rose's life, in contrast to Del's, is made out of modest illuminations and limited victories. Each story is a snapshot of Rose's existence at a particular point in time, and the book avoids the smooth transitions which, in Munro's present view, would violate psychological truth. Yet there is an inner coherence to Rose's character which results from two ingrained habits, exhibited at every stage of life: flight to and from men, and story-telling.

Rose's retreat from her father's wrath is but the first of many abrupt physical movements to which she resorts as a way of handling male dominance. She surrenders to the "violent temptation" to run into Patrick's library carrel and reinstate their engagement; she is frustrated in her efforts to run towards Tom, the Calgary academic, and eventually runs away from the experience of being jilted by Simon, the Queen's academic. As she herself reflects: "she thought...how many overblown excuses she had found, having to leave a place, or being afraid to leave a place, on account of some man". These episodes in most instances suggest not so much a failure of will as a need to acquire self-definition and self-regard through the flattering mirror of a lover. In her two final responses to men (involving Simon, and then Ralph Gillespie, her former schoolmate), Rose shows signs of freeing herself from this pattern of dependence. Running away from Simon represents a disinclination to pine away on the spot, and Rose is eventually rewarded by a renewal of emotional contact with the tangible world. In talking to Ralph, Rose finds a bond of feeling that is not based on "sexual warmth"; recognizing Ralph's self-sufficiency, she moves closer to achieving independence for herself. The book ends with Rose seemingly in a positive frame of mind, though there is no assurance of permanent self-reliance.

Throughout the book, Rose is associated with imitations, acting and story-telling – all seen as expressions of the same psychological impulse. Until the final story, Rose attempts to bolster her feeble self-esteem through acting and story-telling. In essence, however, each of these gestures involves disparagement of self, or of origins, in the act of striving to appear significant. This blend of abasement and theatrics is evident in the royal beatings Rose endures: part of the ritual is that "Rose must play her part in this with the same grossness, the same exaggeration, that her father displays, playing his". In later life, Rose attempts to play the role of Barbara Stanwyck to retain Clifford's interest; she charms people at parties, and acts the parts of interviewer and interviewee with apparent public success, "but sometimes Rose was deeply, unaccountably ashamed". The enterprise of creating an admired but unreal public personality is by its nature humiliating, since it suggests to Rose that her true inner character is either not worthy, or does not exist. Similarly, Rose's stories about her primary school, or about Flo "had considerable effect", but since they record true experiences but are not prompted by sincerity in motivation, "the effect was off-balance".

Yet the positive ending of the book also extends to the aspect we have been examining. On the penultimate page, Rose is said to feel ashamed of her acting, because "she might have been paying attention to the wrong things, reporting antics" - dramatizing herself rather than using the art form as a means of illumination. "That peculiar shame" has, however, been eased by the selfless interchange with Ralph. It is a sign of regeneration in her that she deliberately avoids sullying her feeling for Ralph: "Rose didn't tell this to anybody, glad that there was one thing at least she wouldn't spoil by telling". Rose's self-serving and yet masochistic story-telling seems far removed from Del's ambitious plans as a writer, but both books end with a reminder of the distortions inherent in telling tales.

Since Munro's most recently published work, The Moons of Jupiter (1982), includes material originally destined for Who Do You Think You Are?, it is hardly surprising that the two books have much in common. In many of the The Moons of Jupiter stories, women like Rose, or at least in Rose's situation, find their lives are defined by unsatisfactory but inevitable relationships with predatory men.

A collection of unrelated stories, The Moons of Jupiter nevertheless contains themes that are developed in more than one context. That familiar Munro subject, the attempt to reclaim the past through a return journey, figures in "The Stone in the Field" and "Accident". The frailties of old age, so devastatingly revealed in "Spelling" of Who Do You Think You Are?, are once again unsparingly examined in "Mrs. Cross and Mrs. Kidd", and touched upon in a lighter fashion in "Visitors". The boundaries and limits of puritanism in Huron County are defined in "The Stone in the Field" and "The Turkey Season".

This collection is not, however, dominated by Huron County character types, or even by the return to Huron County of those who survived their childhood in that area. The representative protagonist of the book is a middle-aged woman of unspecified or briefly indicated origins with both a career orientation towards some form of the arts, and a troubled personal life. With variations appropriate to the individual narrative, such a character is central to six ("Dulse", "Bardon Bus", "Prue", "Labor Day Dinner", "Hard-Luck Stories", "The Moons of Jupiter") of the eleven stories. A less gifted writer might be guilty of creating an impression of monotony through the repeated use of similar personality types. Munro's ability to interweave meditation, action, and a variety of settings eliminates this potential problem – the collection has both an appearance of diversity and the depth that results from several approaches to the same issues.

"Dulse" and "Labor Day Dinner" are particularly intriguing and innovative explorations of the pattern just outlined. The former story manages, within the space of scarcely more than twenty pages, to play a dazzling and complex set of variations upon the theme of love. The protagonist, Lydia, has been dumped by a selfish academic lover (most of Munro's scholars are not to be trusted) and flees, as Rose might, to a New Brunswick island (clearly modelled on Grand Manan). There she finds three more male candidates for sexual favours – a young but experienced French Canadian, a wistful middle-aged potato farmer, and their boss, an assertive and vulgar self-made man. Lydia is tempted to indicate her availability either to Eugene, the imploring boy, or Lawrence, the self-confident man of the Maritimes world: "in the past she might have done it....Now it seemed not possible". Lydia's rejection of both the masochism the professor demanded of her and the cold-hearted opportunities open to her on the island heightens her sensitivity to more delicate forms of emotion. She appreciates the rural gentleness of the farmer more than the more overt advances of his companions: she can regard with some nostalgia his loyalty to a culture in which "love is managed for you". She regards with admiration as well as some skepticism a fellow-guest's unquestioning devotion to the memory of Willa Cather, the American novelist who in reality did spend several summers on the island. Mr. Stanley's love for Cather is "a lovely, durable shelter" even if it is erected upon a foundation of sentimentality. It stands in contrast to Lydia's more sophisticated desperation; in another way, Cather's relentless dedication to her craft makes its comment upon Lydia's repudiation of her own claims as a poet.

"Labor Day Dinner" is also a story with much to say about love, but it is not focused upon the perceptions and reactions of a single protagonist. In this story, Munro set herself a formidable technical challenge – to create a wide variety of points of view within the narrow limits of the short story form. At one time or other in the story, the reader is given considerable access to the thoughts of the four guests and the hostess at the dinner party. Munro also ventures into new territory in other ways: George, the sculptor of Hungarian descent is one of the few explicitly non-WASP characters in her fiction; the story is about the strategies of people playing at country living, rather than about the habits of country people. Munro has her customary success on more familiar ground in evoking the imaginations of a girl in late adolescence and her pubescent sister. But the core of the story is built around the contrasting sensibilities of two middle-aged women. Roberta, the victim of middle-aged "subtle withering", feels she has "no clear moments of authority" in living with George – she has given up her work as an illustrator of children's books in order to help him with his endless home improvement schemes. Valerie, the hostess, has been physically unattractive all her days, but thrives in an existence independent of love. Since her husband's death, she has master-minded her own house renovations, and her air of lively self-command contrasts with Roberta's edginess. By the end of the story, Roberta feels that temporarily "she has power" in her relationship with George, but the reader is left with the impression that she, like Lydia, is doomed to be "up and down". In general, the story opposes the volatile emotions of Roberta's household to the more controlled, but also more limited, feelings of Valerie and her daughter Ruth, the inheritor of her virtues. The story presents these two responses to life, making their consequences clear, but not choosing between them. We have noticed temperamental oppositions as a structural principle in such major stories as "Red Dress-1946", "The Peace of Utrecht" and "Memorial". In the broader context of Munro's work, we find Valerie's self-sufficiency, arising out of different causes, in Del Jordan, and Roberta's dependency upon male approval in Rose. It is perhaps legitimate to conjecture that Munro understands and recreates radically opposed types of female emotion because she finds some counter-part to each kind of feeling within herself. She told Hancock, without elaboration, that "I feel that I am two rather different people, two very different women", and elaborated on what seems to be much the same insight in talking to Graeme Gibson, a decade earlier:

> There's the desire to give, even to be dominated, to
> be, at least I, in many ways, want a quite traditional
> role, and then of course the writer stands right
> outside this, and so there's the conflict right there.

The ambivalence Munro feels about being a writer is one of several personal concerns which contribute to the vitality and emotional depth of her fiction. Some of Munro's finest stories express feelings that evoke responses from any sensitive reader, but are at the same time explorations and discoveries of the writer's own emotion, translated into the partial distance fiction provides. Yet Munro is also a gifted objective chronicler of such subjects as the traditional values of her childhood environment, the pathos of old age, and the frantic search in our time for a vanished sense of wholeness. For all her fundamental seriousness, Munro has not forgotten the writer's obligation to give pleasure: her stories attest to her remarkable powers of observation, her unfailing ear for speech of all kinds, and her capacity for the kind of wit which is unsentimental without deserting compassion.

Munro's qualities as a writer have been widely recognized. It requires a substantial research effort to unearth any reviewer or critic who has the slightest reservations about the value of her work. Among the hundreds of reviews in the Calgary collection and at the offices of Munro's current publisher, one comes across a handful of lukewarm notices. American and English reviews are just as uniformly favourable as Canadian ones. Critical articles, a growing stream since the early Seventies, have lately swelled into a torrent. A good sampling, dealing with such matters as Munro's early work, her narrative technique and use of language, and (the best essay in the collection) the "art of disarrangement" in Who Do You Think You Are?, may be found in the volume Probable Fictions: Alice Munro's Narrative Acts, edited by Louis K. MacKendrick.

"I will never, never run out of things to write about" (Hancock interview). We all have reason to hope that Munro will keep this pledge, so that we will continue to have an abundant supply of stories from this versatile, supremely talented and profoundly moving writer.

Note

Interviews quoted in this essay are taken from the following sources (given in chronological order): John Metcalf, Journal of Canadian Fiction, 4 (Fall 1972); Graeme Gibson, Eleven Canadian Novelists (1973); Kem Murch, Chatelaine (August 1975); Alan Twigg, For Openers (1981); J. R. "Tim" Struthers, in Louis K. MacKendrick, ed., Probable Fictions (1983; interview done on April 27, 1981); Geoff Hancock, Canadian Fiction Magazine, 43 (1983).

Archival Introduction

A common criticism of archival repositories is their failure to prepare and publish descriptive inventories beyond brief collection-level entries in guides to repository holdings, or in tools like the Union List of Manuscripts in Canadian Repositories. The absence of such finding aids hampers both researchers and reference staff in their efforts to locate specific items, particularly in extensive collections. Unfortunately, since awareness of and access to primary materials are pre-requisites for many other research projects, including traditional bibliographies, editions of letters, critical studies and biographies, archives are seen as sources of frustration almost as often as they are seen as sources of information.

The University of Calgary's archival inventory series is an attempt to remedy this situation for its Canadian literary archives. Each inventory is primarily a control tool designed to identify the items in a single acquisition and maintain their physical relationships. The inventories will be most useful when used in conjunction with a personal examination of the documents themselves. Researchers and reference staff can now readily locate documents through the organization of the inventory itself, and through a variety of indexed access points. In turn, scholarly citations can be specific and unambiguous.

In a wider context, each inventory will give external researchers an opportunity to examine the structure and content of a particular literary archive in considerable detail, and make informed decisions on the advisability of committing scarce resources to examine the papers in person.

Archival methodology has been followed for arrangement and description, resulting in the standard configuration of collection, series, sub-series, file and item. Original order has been maintained wherever possible. However, private papers rarely have as structured an order as institutional records, nor is it often possible to examine the papers before they arrive in the repository in order to document the filing system as the author used it. More usually, the papers arrive in boxes, where efficient use of space may have taken precedence over original filing. Experience has shown that the file or package represents the highest level of integrity for original order, whether it is a file of letters, or a file of literary manuscripts. Labelled or unidentified, a file's contents reflect most reliably a unit of organization which had intellectual meaning for the author. Although a "file" may be rehoused in several folders for purposes of conservation (where they are identified as follows, MsC XX.1.1-3), file contents are maintained as strictly as possible, with only the most blatant misfiles being removed. It is felt preferable to direct the researcher to idiosyncratically placed items through the index rather than destroy a link which may not be immediately apparent. A coherent internal order is likewise maintained. In the absence of a coherent internal order, an appropriate order is adopted.

The next level of integrity is found in a grouping of files. It is easy to deduce that files relating to one novel were kept together. It is less easy to determine if a sequence of novels was filed alphabetically by title or chronologically by creation. Thus, one can be reasonably sure of order within sub-units, but less sure of how those units were arranged within series. In the absence of an author-imposed order, literary manuscripts are most often arranged chronologically in order to facilitate the addition of subsequent accessions. To aid the researcher, entries for archival series include a note on arrangement.

The relation of series to each other within a collection is most likely to be imposed by the archivist. In our case, correspondence series are always placed first. Manuscript series are most often arranged alphabetically by genre. This avoids the problem of establishing criteria of precedence for poetry, novels, short stories, plays, etc. Occasionally, when the material suggests it, a manuscript series is divided into fiction and non-fiction rather than specific genres.

The only materials removed from collections are published items, such as novels, anthologies, volumes of poetry, etc., which have no annotations beyond a signature. Where the text of such a published work has been annotated, it is kept with the papers since it is judged to have reverted to a draft stage. Items removed from periodicals, individual issues and offprints are also retained with the papers where they can be stored more securely and linked more directly with the author.

It is especially important for the researcher to use the indexes since the observance of original order will sometimes result in a location at variance with major series as identified in the table of contents. In particular, correspondence can be left attached to a manuscript or pasted into a scrapbook, rather than incorporated into the correspondence series proper. An edition of letters might well handle the entries differently, but since these archival inventories parallel exactly the physical arrange- ment of the collections, items could well be missed if the researcher relies solely on the inventory document entries.

Notation is based on a collection/box/folder/item sequence.

Description has been guided by two principles. One, descrip- tion is most useful when it is as free as possible from subjectivity and judgments of researcher interest. Two, it should provide document control for the repository and an acceptable degree of detail for the user.

Since the latter is a matter of opinion, it cannot be re-iterated too strongly that these tools are intended to pave the way for, not usurp the place of, fully annotated editions of letters, definitive textual studies and traditional bibliographies. For this reason, and in the interests of an efficient publication time-line, research external to the collections has been kept to a minimum, and our entries will necessarily fall short of the detailed investigation appropriate to areas of scholarship which are deemed to be outside the repository's archival responsibility.

Entries have been written, therefore, from information contained in the documents themselves. Thus, while we have tried to give the full names of correspondents rather than actual salutations and signatures, we have not hazarded a guess when the geographical location of an outgoing letter is missing or a corporate title is absent, even though both may appear in a previous or subsequent document. Similarly, titles are taken from the manuscript texts and may differ from the published versions. Descriptive comment on textual variations between collection drafts and their published state has not been undertaken. In this respect, researchers should note that, on principle, variant drafts are not separated and/or re-arranged because they fail to match the published work since they may accurately reflect an earlier stage. Establishing the order of creation in the absence of an internal date, accompanying letter or author notation is attempted only in the most obvious instances. The determination of chronology which requires close textual analysis and comparison is best done by the user researching definitive texts. Nonetheless, it is felt that sufficient information has been included in the indexes and entries themselves to allow the user to identify documents and conduct further research.

Descriptive rules are based on an early draft revision of Chapter 4, Anglo-American Cataloguing Rules, 2nd edition (AACR II). This draft revision addressed itself to collection and item levels only. It was felt appropriate, nonetheless, to extend the format to the intervening levels, and thus allow the full archival hierarchy from collection to item to be described within a consistent set of rules. The final version of this draft, which now takes account of all archival levels (p. 1), is available as Archives, Personal Papers and Manuscripts (APPM) by Steven L. Hensen. Besides the advantage of institutional control, full hierarchical description allows researchers to choose a point of entry at the level most useful to them.

Capitalization of titles follows AACR II, but the evolution of the APPM rules has resulted in some discrepancies with the Calgary format. Thus, we continue to include a statement of responsibility for letters. Other variants are dashes and question marks within parentheses where it has been thought necessary to signify absent or doubtful information: _____, John; 1964(?).

Difficulties resulting from item, page and leaf counts have been resolved as follows. Where an entry lacks an item count, but gives a page count, it indicates that itemizing would be misleading; for instance, a unit of reworked pages which includes three versions of a single page. Also certain entries, a notebook, for example, will have a physical item count of "1", but in all probability will contain a number of individual creative items. Both page and leaf counts are given when the count differs; that is, 8 pages on 4 leaves. Entries with page counts only indicate an identical number of leaves. Physical details beyond extent are rare, and are given only where absolutely necessary for identification.

The indexing emphasis has been determined by our reference experience. In order to satisfy the immediate need for information created by researcher interest in the University of Calgary literary archives, a level of indexing the inventories has been chosen which, although not as complete as we would wish, affords access for those users interested primarily in the papers of the principal, while meeting the requirements of users whose main interest lies in the principal's contacts. Entries for correspondence are indexed by both writer and recipient and, where necessary, corporate affiliation. All references to the principal's titles in correspondence are indexed. Enclosures are handled in the same way. In the literary series, all entries for the principal's titles are indexed. However, the research limitations imposed at the descriptive stage are reflected in the title indexing, where there is less cross-referencing than we would have liked.

Users seeking third-party access will find the indexing less satisfactory. No third party names or titles mentioned in correspondence have been indexed. Thus, while Carlos Baker is indexed as a correspondent in the Hugh MacLennan Papers, his reference to Ernest Hemingway is not indexed. Similarly, references to the principal's titles only are indexed; therefore, a letter in the MacLennan Papers from Pierre Berton mentioning The National Dream will be found indexed by his name, but not by the title.

And finally, there is no topical indexing. For example, indexing to Rudy Wiebe's The Temptations of Big Bear will not serve the user whose topic of interest is the North American Indian. Nor will post-modern criticism be indexed in the Robert Kroetsch Papers.

In justification, it is felt that links such as those in the Baker/ Hemingway and Berton/National Dream instances are likely to be made without indexing, and that users searching topically are likely to have sources more appropriate to their needs elsewhere. Given constraints of

economics and time, our primary responsibility must be to users researching the works and immediate contacts of the principal of each collection.

Each inventory forms a segment in an automated database for all
the Canadian authors' papers at the University of Calgary, and these
database records will include a relationship complexity note
(APPM 4.7 B1) and a finding aid note (APPM 4.7 B11) which do not
appear in the published inventories. More significantly, the technology
available for this automation and our desire to co-operate in institutional
networking have served to place unavoidable constraints on the printed
format. Certain descriptive elements, which are necessary in each
discrete electronic record, are repeated in the inventory, where they are
unnecessary; e.g., the repetition of the author's name and birthdate.
Square brackets could not serve their normal descriptive function.
Italicized words could not be underlined. These were felt to be minor
inconveniences when weighed against the immeasurable value of a net-
worked, cumulative database with its possibilities of cross-collection
reference and sort functions. Cross-collection searches are particularly
important for the user interested not so much in the principal authors as
in their contacts, while a computer sort on collection level entries could
provide a current guide to our collection holdings for distribution in
pamphlet form.

*****

Although an early approach had been made to Alice Munro in
1974, the papers described in this inventory could not be acquired by the
University of Calgary until mid-1980, when an agreement was finalized
with Alan H. MacDonald, Director of Libraries.

Initially, Alice Munro wrote that she had not retained "that
many" manuscripts. Fortunately, this proved not to be the case, for
when a trunk and a suitcase were unpacked, there were 2.5 metres of
papers going back to the early 1950s.

No lists accompanied the papers, and some materials were loose.
The disorder was not, as the author suggested, total, but it has
presented challenges with respect to arrangement and description. Alice
Munro herself has been most co-operative in helping us date items, and
confirming many of our identifications.

Manuscript Collection 37, the first consignment of Alice Munro's
literary archives, documents the author's literary period from the early
1950s, when Munro was first submitting short stories to periodicals, to
1979, the year after Munro won the Governor General's Literary Award,
her second, for Who Do You Think You Are?. Represented in the Papers

are correspondence, manuscripts ranging from holograph preliminary drafts to author's proofs, galleys, published stories and reviews. It includes articles and essays by other authors about Munro and her fiction.

Correspondence in the Alice Munro Papers consists of general and personal letters. Personal correspondence (Box 1) is currently closed to researchers. Business letters are from publishers, editors, producers, agents and literary associates; none of Munro's outgoing letters are represented. General correspondence files are arranged alphabetically by corporate or individual correspondent. Letters from readers have been collected in one file, arranged chronologically, at the end of the correspondence series.

All letters enclosing manuscripts have been removed to the correspondence series; where pertinent, repository photocopies replace the original letters in the manuscript files. Letters forwarded by Munro's agent, Virginia Barber, are included in the Virginia Barber file, even if covering letters are absent. The researcher is, therefore, advised to check the index to be certain that all letters from a particular correspondent are located.

Literary manuscripts in the collection are chiefly from the novel and short story genres. The majority of Munro's manuscripts are undated and untitled, and in many cases various drafts and fragments were mixed together when received by the university. Although drafts are seldom paginated, an attempt has been made to sort the material and to pull together fragments from the same or similar drafts. Manuscripts for each title have been rough-sorted chronologically, with drafts closest to the published version filed last. However, it must be emphasized that this is a tentative sort only, and it remains the scholarly task of the researcher to determine the order in which undated material was written and whether fragments filed together actually belong to the same draft.

Fiction manuscripts have been divided into the following series: novel, collected short story (which includes all short stories published in Munro's short story collections), uncollected short story (which includes all other titled short story manuscripts, published, unpublished or fragmentary), notebook and untitled fragment, and television.

The novel series contains manuscripts for Lives of Girls and Women and for an unpublished novel written in the 1960s, which Alice Munro says "never really came to much, though I worked at it". The unpublished novel fragments are variously titled The White Norwegian, The Norwegian and Death of a White Fox. Because the novel is unpublished and the majority of the fragments are untitled, it was necessary to arbitrarily select an uniform title, namely Death of a White

Fox, to pull together the untitled material in the inventory. Titled fragments are entered in the inventory and indexed under the title on the manuscript but indexed as well under the uniform title so that all manuscripts for the novel can be found in the index under the title Death of a White Fox. Fragments from the same or similar versions have been filed together, but again, the sorting is tentative.

A large proportion of Alice Munro's work from the 1960s is related in some degree to the novel Lives of Girls and Women. Manuscripts for this novel are arranged alphabetically by chapter title, with apparently related, untitled material filed with the chapter manuscripts. However, in addition to manuscripts filed under the novel title, a substantial amount of the material in the notebook and untitled fragment series relates somewhat to this novel, and researchers are urged to examine this material, using the title index to locate all related items.

In addition to chapter manuscripts for Lives of Girls and Women, the Papers contain three manuscripts of the novel itself and a partial manuscript about which Alice Munro says, "I was writing Lives as a more conventional novel at one period and then I took the material out and put it into cyclets". Manuscript material is followed by reviews of the novel.

The collected short story series consists of stories in Alice Munro's short story collections published before 1983. Although The Moons of Jupiter had not been published when this accession ended in 1979, stories published in this collection are entered under The Moons of Jupiter to provide consistency in the inventory arrangements of this and the following accessions. The series is arranged chronologically by date of publication under the short story collection titles. Individual stories are entered under the collection title followed by the short story title, e.g., Dance of the Happy Shades : The Peace of Utrecht. Both titles are indexed. Although grouped under the collection title, these individual stories are arranged alphabetically because they do not constitute a "collection" manuscript.

The titles of Munro's novel and short story collections in this accession are all taken from selections within the work, i.e., from either a chapter or short story. To differentiate in the index between these identical titles, either "novel" or "short stories" has been added to the titles of the collected work. For example "Dance of the Happy Shades : short stories" refers to the short story collection; whereas, "Dance of the Happy Shades" refers to the short story contained within the collection.

In order to keep manuscripts for a particular story together, all manuscripts for the same short story have been arranged under the title used in the short story collection even if the title varies. For example, "Day of the Butterfly", in the short story collection Dance of the Happy Shades, was first published in Chatelaine in 1956 as "Goodbye Myra". Material titled "Goodbye Myra" will be found filed with "Day of the Butterfly". All variant titles are indexed under both the variant title and the title used in the short story collection. The researcher can thus find all variant titled material for a particular short story by checking the index under the title used in Munro's short story collections. Where a title varies only in the initial article, for example, "An Ounce of Cure" and "The Ounce of Cure", only the title used in the collected short stories is indexed.

Occasionally Munro uses the same title for several unrelated stories, e.g., "Places at Home". In such cases the index will show, in parentheses following the title, the variant title under which the short story was published, for example, "Places at Home (The Peace of Utrecht)".

Manuscripts for short stories in each collection are followed when present by manuscripts for the entire collection. Included are a manuscript for the collection Something I've Been Meaning to Tell You and a partial manuscript for this collection titled Ten Stories by Alice Munro, which may have been a precursor to the published edition.

Several partial manuscripts for Who Do You Think You Are? are present. These manuscripts were broken up and scattered in Munro's Papers. The manuscripts were pulled together based on the various types of pagination used in the drafts; the type of pagination used to identify the drafts is described in the inventory note area. The researcher should be aware that this consolidation of short stories to produce a collection manuscript is tentative, and it is the responsibility of the researcher to verify the arrangement. Reviews for the collections Dance of the Happy Shades and Something I've Been Meaning to Tell You follow, respectively, manuscripts for those collections.

Also contained in the collected short story series are a number of manuscripts intended as a text for an album of Ontario photographs by Peter D'Angelo. Ms. Munro had not seen the photographs, and the text was unpublished. The collective untitled manuscripts have been arbitrarily titled "Photo Album Text" for descriptive and indexing purposes, and are filed after manuscripts for Who Do You Think You Are? because of the similarity of some of the text to material in that collection.

The uncollected short story series consists of all titled short stories, published or unpublished, complete or fragmentary, not included in Munro's short story collections published before 1983. Manuscript arrangement is alphabetical by title. Similar untitled stories are filed with titled material; the same or similar stories with variant titles are filed together, creating some apparent inconsistency in the alphabetical arrangement. Where variant titles exist, drafts are filed under the published title; for example, the short story published as "Characters" is also often titled "Pleistocene", but all drafts will be filed with the published title "Characters". Cross references are given in the inventory note, and variant titled material is indexed with both published and variant titles.

The notebook and untitled fragment series contains a number of notebooks, dated by Alice Munro in a visit to the University of Calgary in 1981, as well as untitled fragments not closely related to titled material. The notebooks will be of interest to the researcher as Munro does much of her preliminary work in long hand. Furthermore, much of the notebook material written in the 1960s is set in Jubilee and appears to be preliminary work for Lives of Girls and Women.

The untitled fragments have been sorted into two groups: those thought to be written before 1970 and set in rural Ontario and those believed written in the late 1960s and the 1970s and set in urban centres or involving a return to rural Ontario. The judgment is based on story setting and on a comparison of various typewriter founts used. Within each group, manuscripts are described only if sections relate to titled material or if description is warranted by a substantial amount of similar material. Described material is followed in each group by miscellaneous fragments. Where material in the notebook and untitled fragment series appears to be related to titled material, this relationship is described in the inventory note, and the title is indexed.

The television series consists of scripts for 1847 : The Irish, Munro's contribution to The Newcomers/Les Arrivants, a Canadian Broadcasting Corporation drama series on Canadian immigration. "A Better Place Than Home", the prose adaptation of the television drama, is also represented in this series.

A small poetry series consisting of one file and a non-fiction series containing several articles and essays complete the literary manuscript section of the Alice Munro Papers.

A series of interviews, articles and essays written by other authors about Alice Munro and her fiction and a small miscellaneous series complete the inventory.

The inventory for the second accession of Alice Munro's literary archives, covering the period 1973 to 1982, is currently being prepared for publication. A third accession has been received.

When the second accession, Manuscript Collection 38, was being arranged, it was discovered that two partial manuscripts for the collection

<u>Who Do You Think You Are</u>? in the first accession were part of a larger collection manuscript in the second accession. In order to consolidate this collection manuscript, the related material was moved from the first to the second accession. Similarly, a manuscript of the short story "Providence" was transferred from accession two to accession one to consolidate a collection manuscript. Where transfers of manuscripts between accessions occur, the transfer is indicated in the inventory note area for the particular manuscript.

Jean M. Moore
Jean F. Tener

Abbreviations

A.D.S.--autograph document(s) signed by the writer of the text

A.L.--autograph letter(s)

A.L.S.--autograph letter(s) signed by the hand of the author

A.M.S.--autograph memorandum signed by the hand of the author

D.--document(s)

D.S.--document(s) signed

L.S.--letter(s) signed; signature only in the hand of the author

s.l.--sine loco

s.n.--sine nomine

T.L.--typed letter(s) lacking signature

T.L.S.--typed letter(s) signed by the author

T.D.--typed document(s) lacking signature

T.D.S.--typed document(s) signed

T.M.--typed memo(s) lacking signature

T.M.S.--typed memo(s) signed by the hand of the author

Archival Inventory

MUNRO, ALICE, 1931–   MsC 37
PAPERS, CA. 1950-1979.

2.5 METRES : 2073 ITEMS.
AUTHOR; b. ALICE LAIDLAW.
CONSISTS OF FOLLOWING SERIES: CORRESPONDENCE
(1954-1978); NOVEL (CA. 1960-1978); COLLECTED SHORT
STORY (CA. 1950-1978); UNCOLLECTED SHORT STORY
(CA. 1950-197-); NOTEBOOK AND UNTITLED FRAGMENT
(CA. 1950-1978); TELEVISION (CA. 1976-1978); POETRY
(N.D.); NON-FICTION (CA. 1962-1978); WORKS ON
ALICE MUNRO (1957-1979); AND MISCELLANEOUS
(N.D., 1961-1975).

MUNRO, ALICE, 1931–   Msc 37.2
CORRESPONDENCE SERIES, 1954-1978.

160 ITEMS.
LETTERS FROM EDITORS, PUBLISHERS, PRODUCERS,
AGENTS AND OTHER ASSOCIATES IN THE LITERARY,
PUBLISHING AND MEDIA FIELDS. ARRANGED
ALPHABETICALLY BY CORRESPONDENT WITH THE
EXCEPTION OF THE LAST TWO FILES WHICH CONTAIN
TWO BRIEF NOTES BY A. MUNRO AND READERS'
CONGRATULATORY MESSAGES. ITEMS WITHIN FILES
ARRANGED CHRONOLOGICALLY. CONTRACTS AND
ROYALTY STATEMENTS WHEN PRESENT ARE INCLUDED
IN CORRESPONDENCE FILES.

APPLETON CENTURY CROFTS.   Msc 37.2.1
    Letter (1961 September 26), New York, N.Y., from
    Theodore M. Purdy, Editor-in-Chief, Appleton
    Century Crofts, to Alice Munro, West Vancouver,
    B.C.

    1 item : 1 p.
    T.L.S. rejecting unidentified short stories, and
    discussing difficulty in selling short story
    collections.

ASSOCIATION OF CANADIAN UNIVERSITY TEACHERS   Msc 37.2.2
    OF ENGLISH.
    Letter (1978 April 19), Edmonton, Alta., from Juliet
    McMaster, President, ACUTE, to Alice Munro,
    Clinton, Ont.

    1 item : 1 p.
    A.L.S. regarding A. Munro's participation in a
    conference at the University of Western Ontario.

AUSTRALIA. HIGH COMMISSION (CANADA).   Msc 37.2.3
    Invitation (1978(?) March 15), Ottawa, Ont., from
    His Excellency John Ryan, Australian High
    Commissioner, and Mrs. Ryan to Mr. and Mrs.
    Gerald Fremlin.

    1 item : 1 p.
    Typescript and holograph dinner invitation.

BABINEAU, NICOLE.   MsC 37.2.4
    Letter (1978 January 9), Brownsburg, P.Q., from
    N. Babineau to Alice Munro.

    1 item : 1 p.
    T.L.S. regarding attempts to have N. Babineau's
    French translation of Dance of the happy shades
    published.

BODSWORTH, FRED.   MsC 37.2.5
    Letter (1974 October 31), Toronto, Ont., from
    F. Bodsworth to Alice Munro.

    1 item : 2 p.
    T.L.S. recommending a New York agent for
    A. Munro, and mentioning Lives of girls and women
    and Something I've been meaning to tell you.
    Unidentified holograph note and phone numbers on
    verso.

BRITISH COLUMBIA LIBRARY ASSOCIATION.   MsC 37.2.6
    Letter (1972 September 29), Vancouver, B.C., from
    Bryan L. Bacon, B.C. Authors' Day Committee,
    British Columbia Library Association, to Alice Munro,
    Victoria, B.C.

    1 item : 2 p.
    T.L.S. discussing arrangements for the Association's
    award presentation to A. Munro as outstanding
    British Columbia fiction writer, and listing award
    winners in other categories.

CANADA COUNCIL.   MsC 37.2.7
    Letter (1969 May 13), and application forms from
    Canada Council to Alice Munro.

    3 items : 7 p.
    Letter regarding Governor General's Literary Award
    and two blank application forms for arts scholarship.
    Application forms not itemized.

Martineau, Jean.   MsC 37.2.7.1
    Letter (1969 May 13), Ottawa, Ont., from
    J. Martineau, Chairman, Canada Council,
    to Alice Munro, Victoria, B.C.

    1 p.
    T.L.S. enclosing cash prize accompanying
    the Governor General's Literary Award for
    1968.

CANADIAN BROADCASTING CORPORATION.   MsC 37.2.8
    Letters and contracts (1954-1976 June 21), from
    various CBC officials, chiefly Robert Weaver, to
    Alice Munro.

    15 items : 23 p.
    Letters discussing publication, radio and television
    production of several of A. Munro's short stories.
    Includes two contracts for radio productions.

        Canadian Broadcasting Corporation.   MsC 37.2.8.1
            Contract (1954), between CBC and Alice
            Munro, North Vancouver, B.C.

            4 p.
            T.D.S. (carbon copy) listing terms for
            radio production of The strangers on the
            program Trans-Canada Matinee. Signed by
            T. G. Falconer for CBC.

        Canadian Broadcasting Corporation.   MsC 37.2.8.2
            Contract (1955?), between CBC and Alice
            Munro, North Vancouver, B.C.

            4 p.
            T.D.S. (carbon copy) listing terms for
            radio broadcast of The idyllic summer on
            the program Anthology. Signed by Charlie
            Frick for CBC. Discrepancy in dates on
            the contract.

Weaver, Robert.   MsC 37.2.8.3
    Letter (1958 December 12), Toronto, Ont.,
    from R. Weaver, Canadian Broadcasting
    Corporation, to Alice Munro, West
    Vancouver, B.C.

    1 p.
    T.L.S. giving advice regarding Canada
    Council fellowship application.

Weaver, Robert.   MsC 37.2.8.4
    Letter (1961 August 24), Toronto, Ont.,
    from R. Weaver, Program Officer, Special
    Programs, Canadian Broadcasting
    Corporation, to Alice Munro, West
    Vancouver, B.C.

    1 p.
    T.L.S. discussing several possibilities,
    including Tamarack Review, for publication
    of A. Munro's short stories.

Weaver, Robert.   MsC 37.2.8.5
    Letter (1961 August 29), Toronto, Ont.,
    from R. Weaver, Program Officer, Special
    Programs, Canadian Broadcasting
    Corporation, to Alice Munro, West
    Vancouver, B.C.

    1 p.
    T.L.S. (carbon copy) forwarding reviews
    of the anthology Canadian short stories
    edited by R. Weaver.

Todd, Lyon.   MsC 37.2.8.6
    Letter (1961 September 26), Toronto,
    Ont., from L. Todd, Story Editor,
    Television Drama, Canadian Broadcasting
    Corporation, to Alice Munro, Vancouver,
    B.C.

    1 p.
    T.L.S. inquiring if A. Munro would be
    interested in writing or adapting material
    for television drama series Playdate.

Weaver, Robert.   MsC 37.2.8.7
    Letter (1961 November 8), Toronto, Ont.,
    from R. Weaver, Program Officer, Special
    Programs, Canadian Broadcasting
    Corporation, to Alice Munro, Vancouver,
    B.C.

    1 p.
    T.L.S. discussing possibilities for
    publication of A. Munro's short stories,
    and suggesting The Peace of Utrecht for
    inclusion in an anthology which R. Weaver
    is preparing.

Weaver, Robert.   MsC 37.2.8.8
    Letter (1961 November 22), Toronto, Ont.,
    from R. Weaver, Program Officer, Special
    Programs, Canadian Broadcasting
    Corporation, to Alice Munro, West
    Vancouver, B.C.

    1 p.
    T.L.S. discussing inclusion of The Peace
    of Utrecht in the Faber anthology and
    other publishing possibilities.

Weaver, Robert.   MsC 37.2.8.9
    Letter (1968 November 5), Toronto, Ont.,
    from R. Weaver, Assistant Radio Network
    Supervisor, Drama and Special Programs,
    Canadian Broadcasting Corporation, to
    Alice Munro, Victoria, B.C.

    1 p.
    T.L.S. enclosing review, and requesting a
    short story submission for radio program
    Anthology.

Weaver, Robert.   MsC 37.2.8.10
    Letter (1973 March 28), Toronto, Ont.,
    from R. Weaver, Head, Radio Arts
    Programming, Canadian Broadcasting
    Corporation, to Alice Munro, Victoria,
    B.C.

    1 p.
    T.L.S. enclosing manuscript of
    Forgiveness in families (MsC 37.7.35), and
    requesting short story submission for
    Tamarack Review. R. Weaver refers to a
    "program", possibly broadcast of
    Forgiveness in families on Anthology,
    March 10, 1973.

Weaver, Robert.   MsC 37.2.8.11
    Letter (1973 April 18), Toronto, Ont.,
    from R. Weaver, Head, Radio Arts
    Programming, Canadian Broadcasting
    Corporation, to Alice Munro, Victoria,
    B.C.

    1 p.
    T.L.S. discussing A. Munro's Toronto trip
    and a television drama series involving
    Canadian authors.

Jonas, George.   MsC 37.2.8.12
    Letter (1973 April 25), Toronto, Ont.,
    from G. Jonas, Producer, Television
    Drama, Canadian Broadcasting Corporation,
    to Alice Munro, Victoria, B.C.

    2 p.
    T.L.S. requesting a short story or
    teleplay submission for the Canadian drama
    series The play's the thing.

Weaver, Robert.   MsC 37.2.8.13
    Letter (1974 September 18), Toronto,
    Ont., from R. Weaver, Head, Radio Arts,
    Canadian Broadcasting Corporation, to
    Alice Munro, London, Ont.

    1 p.
    T.L.S. regarding the position of
    writer-in-residence at Carlton University.

Locke, Jeannine.   MsC 37.2.8.14
Letter (1974 September 20), Toronto,
Ont., from J. Locke, Producer, Arts and
Science, Canadian Broadcasting
Corporation, to Alice Munro, London, Ont.

2 p.
T.L.S. inquiring if A. Munro would be
interested in participating in an interview
television series People of our time.

Weaver, Robert.   MsC 37.2.8.15
Letter (1976 June 21), Toronto, Ont.,
from R. Weaver, Head, Radio Arts
Programming, Canadian Broadcasting
Corporation, to Alice Munro, Clinton, Ont.

1 p.
T.L.S. enclosing manuscripts of Privilege
for revision, and mentioning other topics.

CAROUSEL PLAYERS.   MsC 37.2.9
Letter and invitation (1977), from Patricia Mahoney,
Carousel Players, to Alice Munro.

2 items : 40 p. on 37 leaves.
Letter, enclosed play manuscript and theatre
program, all related to production of Mirror!
mirror! by P. Mahoney.

Mahoney, Patricia.   MsC 37.2.9.1
Letter (1977?), St. Catharines, Ont., from
P. Mahoney, Carousel Players, to Alice
Munro.

1 p.
A.L.S. enclosing and asking approval for
P. Mahoney's play Mirror! mirror!, which
includes adapted excerpts from A. Munro's
novel Lives of girls and women and short
stories Executioners, Day of the butterfly
and Red dress-1946. Includes Mirror!
mirror! script. 37 p. on 35 leaves,
typescript (mimeograph) with holograph
revisions.

Carousel Players.   Msc 37.2.9.2
    Invitation (1977 April 16), St. Catharines,
    Ont., from Carousel Players to Alice
    Munro.

    2 p. on 1 leaf.
    Invitation for opening night performance of
    Patricia Mahoney's Mirror! mirror!.

COLLIER, E. C.   Msc 37.2.10
    Letter (1973 September 14), Victoria B.C., from
    E. C. Collier to Alice Munro, Victoria, B.C.

    1 item : 3 p. on 2 leaves.
    T.L.S. expressing appreciation for A. Munro's
    comments on Diana Collier's short story. Encloses
    letter (n.d.), from Vera Collier to A. Munro, also
    expressing appreciation. 2 p. on 1 leaf. A.L.S.

COMMCEPT PUBLISHING LTD.   Msc 37.2.11
    Letter (1978 February 27), Vancouver, B.C., from
    Edward Peck, English Editor, Commcept Publishing
    Ltd., to Alice Munro, Clinton, Ont.

    1 item : 1 p.
    T.L.S. (photocopy) enclosing unidentified
    proofsheets. (Possibly proofsheets for The office
    and/or A. Munro's commentary On writing "The
    office", both published by Commcept Publishing Ltd.
    in Transitions II : short fiction : a source book of
    Canadian literature/edited by E. Peck, 1978.)

COOK, D. E.   Msc 37.2.12
    Letter (1975 March 7), Oakville, Ont., from
    D. E. Cook to Alice Munro.

    1 item : 10 p.
    A.L.S. requesting permission to publish a
    bibliography titled Alice Munro : a checklist.
    Encloses bibliography. 9 p. typescript (photocopy).

ELIZABETH II, QUEEN OF THE UNITED KINGDOM.   Msc 37.2.13
    Certificate (1977), Ottawa, Ont., from Elizabeth II,
    Queen of the United Kingdom, to Alice Munro.

    1 item : 1 p.
    Certificate accompanying medal, probably Silver
    Jubilee Medal, presented to Alice Munro. Signed by
    His Excellency Jules Léger, Governor General of
    Canada.

FAGGETTER, RACHEL.   Msc 37.2.14
    Letter (1978 January 25), Parkville, Australia, from
    R. Faggetter to Alice Munro.

    1 item : 1 p.
    A.L.S. congratulating A. Munro on winning the
    Canada-Australia Literary Prize, and requesting a
    meeting during Australian trip.

FERGUSON, TED.   Msc 37.2.15
    Letter (1970 October 17), Vancouver, B.C., from
    T. Ferguson to Alice Munro, Victoria, B.C.

    1 item : 2 p.
    T.L.S. requesting a letter of recommendation for a
    Canada Council grant, and providing biographical
    information.

GENERAL PUBLISHING CO. LIMITED.   Msc 37.2.16
    Letter (1972 November 29), Don Mills, Ont., from
    Jack Stoddart, President, General Publishing Co.
    Ltd., to Alice Munro, Victoria, B.C.

    1 item : 1 p.
    T.L.S. inquiring if A. Munro would be interested in
    having her first two books, probably Dance of the
    happy shades and Lives of girls and women,
    included in General Publishing's PaperJacks program.

GREAT LAKES COLLEGES ASSOCIATION.   MsC 37.2.17
Letter (1974 May 28), Greencastle, Ind., from
Elizabeth Christman, Coordinator, GLCA New Writer
Awards, to Alice Munro, London, Ont.

1 item : 1 p.
T.L.S. congratulating A. Munro on winning the
GLCA New Writer Award, and discussing
arrangements to visit participating colleges.

HOLT, RINEHART AND WINSTON.   MsC 37.2.18
Letter (1977 July 12), New York, N.Y., from Ellen
Datlow, Assistant to Tom Wallace, Holt, Rinehart and
Winston, to Alice Munro, New York, N.Y.

1 item : 1 p.
T.L.S. expressing praise for short story The beggar
maid, and inquiring about future literary intentions.

LIBERTY.   MsC 37.2.19
Rejection slip (n.d.), Toronto, Ont., from the
Editors, Liberty.

1 item : 1 p.
Typescript form letter rejecting unidentified
manuscript. Includes unidentified holograph
annotations "Thank you, but" and "superb".

MACMILLAN OF CANADA.   MsC 37.2.20
Letters (1974 June 18-1978 April 28), from Macmillan
of Canada officials, chiefly Douglas M. Gibson, to
Alice Munro.

7 items : 12 p.
Letters concerning publication of various short
stories, and relating to A. Munro's text for Peter
D'Angelo's book of photographs.

Neale, Gladys E.   MsC 37.2.20.1
    Letter (1974 June 18), Toronto, Ont.,
    from G. E. Neale, Director, Educational
    Division, Macmillan of Canada, to Alice
    Munro, London, Ont.

    1 p.
    T.L.S. related to publication of How I met
    my husband.

Gibson, Douglas M.   MsC 37.2.20.2
    Letter (1974 August 26), Toronto, Ont.,
    from D. M. Gibson, Editorial Director,
    Trade Division, Macmillan of Canada, to
    Alice Munro, London, Ont.

    2 p.
    T.L.S., with holograph postscript,
    praising short story collection Something
    I've been meaning to tell you, and
    discussing A. Munro's recent radio
    interview.

Gibson, Douglas M.   MsC 37.2.20.3
    Letter (1975 January 23), Toronto, Ont.,
    from D. M. Gibson, Editorial Director,
    Trade Division, Macmillan of Canada, to
    Alice Munro, London, Ont.

    1 p.
    T.L.S. offering a contract for A. Munro's
    next work of fiction, and mentioning album
    of photographs by Peter D'Angelo for
    which A. Munro is writing the text.
    Includes A. Munro's holograph annotations
    of telephone numbers.

Gibson, Douglas M.   MsC 37.2.20.4
    Letter (1975 October 9), Toronto, Ont.,
    from D. M. Gibson, Editorial Director,
    Trade Division, Macmillan of Canada, to
    Alice Munro, Clinton, Ont.

    2 p.
    T.L.S. discussing concerns about Peter
    D'Angelo's photography album for which
    A. Munro is writing the text.

Gibson, Douglas M.   MsC 37.2.20.5
    Letter (1975 December 23), Toronto, Ont.,
    from D. M. Gibson, Editorial Director,
    Trade Division, Macmillan of Canada, to
    Alice Munro, Clinton, Ont.

    2 p.
    T.L.S. discussing the text for Peter
    D'Angelo's album of photographs and
    various other topics.

Gibson, Douglas M.   MsC 37.2.20.6
    Letter (1976 February 4), Toronto, Ont.,
    from D. M. Gibson, Editorial Director,
    Trade Division, Macmillan of Canada, to
    Alice Munro, Clinton, Ont.

    1 p.
    T.L.S. discussing current short stories,
    and requesting that A. Munro read the
    galleys for Jack Hodgins's collection of
    short stories which Macmillan is
    publishing.

Gibson, Douglas M.   MsC 37.2.20.7
    Letter (1978 April 28), Toronto, Ont.,
    from D. M. Gibson, Editorial Director,
    Trade Division, Macmillan of Canada, to
    Alice Munro, Clinton, Ont.

    3 p.
    T.L.S. discussing possible titles and order
    of short stories for next collection,
    probably Who do you think you are?.
    Mentions The beggar maid, Royal beatings,
    Accident, Chaddeleys and Flemings,
    Characters and collection Something I've
    been meaning to tell you. Also mentions
    publication of A. Munro's father's book.

MALASPINA COLLEGE.   MsC 37.2.21
    Letter (1977 September 8), Nanaimo, B.C., from
    Kevin Roberts, Department of English, Malaspina
    College, to Alice Munro, Clinton, Ont.

    1 item : 1 p.
    T.L.S. arranging for A. Munro's reading at
    Malaspina College.

MCCLELLAND AND STEWART LIMITED.   MsC 37.2.22
Letters (1961 October 12-1978 February 15), from
individuals associated with McClelland and Stewart
Limited to Alice Munro.

3 items : 4 p.
Letters concerning attempts to publish short story
collections, and relating to publication of The
newcomers : inhabiting a new land.

McClelland, Jack.   MsC 37.2.22.1
Letter (1961 October 12), Toronto, Ont.,
from J. McClelland, McClelland and Stewart
Limited, to Alice Munro, West Vancouver,
B.C.

2 p.
T.L.S. discussing the marketing problems
of short story collections, and
recommending a novel as A. Munro's first
published work.

Kane, Hugh.   MsC 37.2.22.2
Letter (1961 November 15), Toronto, Ont.,
from H. Kane, McClelland and Stewart
Limited, to Alice Munro, West Vancouver,
B.C.

1 p.
T.L.S. acknowledging A. Munro's decision
to publish a novel before a short story
collection.

Wahl, Charis.   MsC 37.2.22.3
Letter (1978 February 15), Toronto, Ont.,
from C. Wahl, Senior Editor, McClelland
and Stewart Limited, to Alice Munro,
Clinton, Ont.

1 p.
T.L.S. acknowledging receipt of
manuscript later titled A better place than
home, part of The newcomers : inhabiting
a new land.

MCGRAW-HILL BOOK COMPANY.   MsC 37.2.23
    Letters (1973 February 8-1974 May 2), from
    McGraw-Hill Book Company officials, chiefly Joyce
    Johnson, to Alice Munro.

    7 items : 11 p.
    Letters relating to American publication of Lives of
    girls and women and Dance of the happy shades and
    to A. Munro's winning the Great Lakes Colleges
    Association New Writer Award.

        Showalter, Elaine.   MsC 37.2.23.1
            Letter (1973 February 8), London,
            England, from E. Showalter to Joyce
            Johnson, McGraw-Hill Book Company, New
            York, N.Y.

            1 p.
            A.L.S. (photocopy) commenting on Lives
            of girls and women, and mentioning
            E. Showalter's current writing projects.

        Loo, Beverly Jane.   MsC 37.2.23.2
            Letter (1973 February 28), New York,
            N.Y., from B. J. Loo, Manager,
            Subsidiary Rights, McGraw-Hill Book
            Company, to Alice Munro, Victoria, B.C.

            1 p.
            T.L.S. announcing that Book-of-the-Month
            Club, Inc. will feature Lives of girls and
            women as an alternate selection, and
            stating terms.

        Johnson, Joyce.   MsC 37.2.23.3
            Letter (1973 March 6), New York, N.Y.,
            from J. Johnson, McGraw-Hill Book
            Company, to Alice Munro, Victoria, B.C.

            1 p.
            T.L.S. enclosing reviews, probably of
            Lives of girls and women.

Johnson, Joyce.   MsC 37.2.23.4
    Letter (1973 April 2), New York, N.Y.,
    from J. Johnson, McGraw-Hill Book
    Company, to Alice Munro, Victoria, B.C.

    1 p.
    T.L.S. enclosing reviews, probably of
    Lives of girls and women, and
    recommending an agent.

Johnson, Joyce.   MsC 37.2.23.5
    Letter (1973 August 24), New York, N.Y.,
    from J. Johnson, Senior Editor,
    McGraw-Hill Book Company, to Alice
    Munro, Victoria, B.C.

    1 p.
    T.L.S. enclosing review of Lives of girls
    and women, and mentioning publication of
    Dance of the happy shades.

Johnson, Joyce.   MsC 37.2.23.6
    Letter (1973 October 15), New York,
    N.Y., from J. Johnson, McGraw-Hill Book
    Company, to Alice Munro, Victoria, B.C.

    1 p.
    T.L.S. enclosing reviews, and mentioning
    second collection of short stories, probably
    Something I've been meaning to tell you.

Johnson, Joyce.   MsC 37.2.23.7
   Letter (1974 May 2), New York, N.Y.,
   from J. Johnson, McGraw-Hill Book
   Company, to Alice Munro, Scarborough,
   Ont.

   1 p.
   T.L.S. announcing that A. Munro has won
   the Great Lakes Colleges Association New
   Writer Award for Dance of the happy
   shades. Includes letter (1974 April 24),
   Ann Arbor, Mich., from Laurence Barrett,
   President, Great Lakes Colleges
   Association, to J. Johnson, Senior Editor,
   McGraw-Hill Book Company, New York,
   N.Y., announcing the award. 2 p.
   T.L.S. (photocopy); information sheet
   regarding award. 2 p. typescript
   (photocopy).

MCGRAW-HILL COMPANY OF CANADA LIMITED.   MsC 37.2.24
   Letters (1970 December 14-1971 March 23), from
   McGraw-Hill Company of Canada Limited officials to
   Alice Munro.

   3 items : 4 p.
   Letters relating to publication of Lives of girls and
   women and possible paperback edition of Dance of
   the happy shades.

   Coffin, Audrey.   MsC 37.2.24.1
      Letter (1970 December 14), Scarborough,
      Ont., from A. Coffin, McGraw-Hill
      Company of Canada Limited, to Alice
      Munro, Victoria, B.C.

      1 p.
      T.L.S. acknowledging receipt of
      manuscript for Real life, later titled Lives
      of girls and women. Signed "Audrey",
      probably A. Coffin.

Kiil, Toivo.   MsC 37.2.24.2
    Letter (1971 March 10), Scarborough,
    Ont., from T. Kiil, Editor-in-Chief, Trade
    Department, McGraw-Hill Company of
    Canada Limited, to Alice Munro, Victoria,
    B.C.

    1 p.
    T.L.S. enclosing contracts for publication
    of Real life, later titled Lives of girls and
    women, and mentioning Dance of the happy
    shades.

Kiil, Toivo.   MsC 37.2.24.3
    Letter (1971 March 23), Scarborough,
    Ont., from T. Kiil, Editor-in-Chief, Trade
    Division, McGraw-Hill Company of Canada
    Limited, to Alice Munro, Victoria, B.C.

    2 p.
    T.L.S. discussing possibilities for
    American publication of Real life, later
    titled Lives of girls and women, and
    paperback publication of Dance of the
    happy shades.

MCGRAW-HILL RYERSON LIMITED.   MsC 37.2.25
    Letters (1972 October 13-1977 September 8), from
    McGraw-Hill Ryerson Limited officials to Alice Munro.

    9 items : 17 p.
    Letters relating chiefly to publication of Dance of the
    happy shades, Lives of girls and women and
    Something I've been meaning to tell you.

Kiil, Toivo.   MsC 37.2.25.1
        Letter (1972 October 13), Scarborough,
        Ont., from T. Kiil, Editor, Trade
        Division, McGraw-Hill Ryerson Limited, to
        Alice Munro, Victoria, B.C.

        2 p.
        T.L.S. discussing serialization, United
        Kingdom and paperback publication of, and
        various other topics related to, Lives of
        girls and women; also discussing
        paperback publications of Dance of the
        happy shades. Encloses reviews, one with
        holograph note from Harold McGraw,
        McGraw-Hill Book Company, to John
        Macmillan, McGraw-Hill Ryerson Limited.
        2 p. typescript (photocopy).

Kiil, Toivo.   MsC 37.2.25.2
        Letter (1972 November 13), Scarborough,
        Ont., from T. Kiil, Editor, Trade
        Division, McGraw-Hill Ryerson Limited, to
        Alice Munro, Victoria, B.C.

        2 p.
        T.L.S. enclosing payment for publication
        of Red dress, also titled Red dress-1946,
        in McCall's, and relating publication update
        on Dance of the happy shades and Lives of
        girls and women.

Stinson, Jean.   MsC 37.2.25.3
        Letter (1973 April 11), Scarborough, Ont.,
        from J. Stinson, Sponsoring Editor,
        Ryerson Educational Division, McGraw-Hill
        Ryerson Limited, to Alice Munro, Victoria,
        B.C.

        2 p.
        T.L.S. enclosing copy of Day of the
        butterfly (MsC 37.6.12), and requesting
        deletions before publication in language
        text series The world of language.

Kiil, Toivo.   MsC 37.2.25.4
    Letter (1974 September 3), Scarborough,
    Ont., from T. Kiil, Publisher, General
    Books Division, McGraw-Hill Ryerson
    Limited, to Alice Munro, London, Ont.

    2 p.
    T.L.S. enclosing royalty cheque, and
    discussing sales and possible British
    publication of Something I've been meaning
    to tell you, as well as mass market rights
    for Dance of the happy shades.

Coffin, Audrey.   MsC 37.2.25.5
    Letter (1974 October 7), Scarborough,
    Ont., from A. Coffin, McGraw-Hill Ryerson
    Limited, to Alice Munro.

    1 p.
    T.L.S. enclosing manuscript of Something
    I've been meaning to tell you, mentioning
    Forgiveness in families and various other
    topics. Includes holograph annotation
    "Registered". Signed "Audrey", probably
    A. Coffin.

Kiil, Toivo.   MsC 37.2.25.6
    Letter (1975 March 7), Scarborough, Ont.,
    from T. Kiil, Publisher, General Books
    Division, McGraw-Hill Ryerson Limited, to
    Alice Munro, London, Ont.

    2 p.
    T.L.S. enclosing royalty cheque,
    discussing television production of
    Baptizing, paperback edition of Something
    I've been meaning to tell you and contract
    offer for next book.

Byam, Barbara.   MsC 37.2.25.7
    Letter (1975 August 18), Scarborough,
    Ont., from B. Byam, Publisher, Trade
    Books, McGraw-Hill Ryerson Limited, to
    Alice Munro, Clinton, Ont.

    1 p.
    T.L.S. enclosing royalty cheque, and
    discussing editorial policy for future
    works. Holograph list on verso.

Gray, Marilyn.   MsC 37.2.25.8
    Letter (1977 March 3), from M. Gray,
    Manager, Rights and Permissions,
    McGraw-Hill Ryerson Limited, to Patricia
    Mahoney, Carousel Players,
    St. Catharines, Ont.

    1 p.
    T.L.S. (carbon copy) regarding clearance
    of rights for P. Mahoney to use material
    from Dance of the happy shades,
    Something I've been meaning to tell you
    and Lives of girls and women in
    dramatization, probably Mirror! mirror!.

Gray, Marilyn.   MsC 37.2.25.9
    Letter (1977 September 8), Scarborough,
    Ont., from M. Gray, Manager, Rights and
    Permissions, McGraw-Hill Ryerson Limited,
    to Nicole Babineau, Argenteuil, P.Q.

    1 p.
    T.L.S. (photocopy) discussing
    N. Babineau's request to translate
    A. Munro's books. Encloses letter (1977
    August 31), Argenteuil, P.Q., from
    N. Babineau to McGraw-Hill Ryerson
    Limited, Scarborough, Ont., regarding
    request. 1 p. T.L.S. (photocopy).
    Enclosed letter mentions Dance of the
    happy shades and N. Babineau's thesis on
    A. Munro's fiction.

MCLEAN, ROSS.   MsC 37.2.26
    Letters (1971 December 3-1971 December 21), from
    R. McLean to Alice Munro.

    2 items : 3 p.
    Letters relating to possible television production of
    Lives of girls and women.

        McLean, Ross.   MsC 37.2.26.1
            Letter (1971 December 3), Toronto, Ont.,
            from R. McLean to Alice Munro.

            2 p.
            T.L.S. expressing interest in producing
            A. Munro's novel, probably Lives of girls
            and women, as a television film.

        McLean, Ross.   MsC 37.2.26.2
            Letter (1971 December 21), Toronto, Ont.,
            from R. McLean to Alice Munro.

            1 p.
            T.L.S. discussing possibilities for
            television production of Lives of girls and
            women.

MONTREALER.   MsC 37.2.27
    Letters (1961 August 17-1962 June 8), from Gerald
    Taafe, Editor, Montrealer, to Alice Munro.

    3 items : 3 p.
    Letters related to publication of Remember Roger
    Mortimer and The office.

        Taaffe, Gerald.   MsC 37.2.27.1
            Letter (1961 August 17), Montreal, P.Q.,
            from G. Taafe, Editor, Montrealer, to Alice
            Munro, West Vancouver, B.C.

            1 p.
            T.L.S. requesting short story or other
            submissions for publication in the
            Montrealer.

Taaffe, Gerald.   MsC 37.2.27.2
Letter (1961 November 15), Montreal,
P.Q., from G. Taaffe, Editor, Montrealer,
to Alice Munro, West Vancouver, B.C.

1 p.
T.L.S. relating that the Montrealer will
publish Remember Roger Mortimer? in the
February 1962 issue.

Taaffe, Gerald.   MsC 37.2.27.3
Letter (1962 June 8), Montreal, P.Q., from
G. Taaffe, Editor, Montrealer, to Alice
Munro, West Vancouver, B.C.

1 p.
T.L.S. relating that The office will be
published in the September 1962 issue of
the Montrealer.

MS.   MsC 37.2.28
Letter (1973 March 2), New York, N.Y., from Nina
Finkelstein, Editor, Ms., to Alice Munro.

1 item : 1 p.
T.L.S. praising Lives of girls and women, and
requesting submission of short stories for possible
publication in Ms.

MUSSON BOOK COMPANY.   MsC 37.2.29
Letter (1972 September 21), Don Mills, Ont., from
Allan J. Stormont, Supervisor, Advertising and Sales
Promotion, Musson Book Company, to Alice Munro,
Victoria, B.C.

1 item : 1 p.
T.L.S. discussing the introduction, written by
A. Munro, for reprint of The school of femininity by
Margaret Lawrence Greene.

NEW YORKER.   MsC 37.2.30
    Letters (1976 November 18-1978 February 6), from
    Charles McGrath, New Yorker, to Alice Munro.

    6 items : 9 p.
    Letters and letter fragments related to publication of
    Royal beatings, The beggar maid and The moons of
    Jupiter and to rejection of Simon's luck and
    Chaddeleys and Flemings.

        McGrath, Charles.   MsC 37.2.30.1
            Letter (1976 November 18), New York,
            N.Y., from C. McGrath, New Yorker, to
            Alice Munro, Clinton, Ont.

            3 p.
            T.L.S. discussing publication of Royal
            beatings, and relating New Yorker editorial
            policy.

        New Yorker.   MsC 37.2.30.2
            Letter fragment (1976 December 21), New
            York, N.Y., from New Yorker to Alice
            Munro.

            1 p.
            Typescript letter fragment, probably from
            Charles McGrath, discussing editing of
            Royal beatings, and expressing interest in
            publishing The beggar maid.

        McGrath, Charles.   MsC 37.2.30.3
            Letter (1977 January 11), New York,
            N.Y., from C. McGrath, New Yorker, to
            Alice Munro, Clinton, Ont.

            2 p.
            T.L.S. enclosing galleys of Royal beatings
            (MsC 37.11.9), and discussing editing of
            Royal beatings and The beggar maid for
            publication in the New Yorker.

McGrath, Charles.   MsC 37.2.30.4
    Letter (1977 August 3), New York, N.Y.,
    from C. McGrath, New Yorker, to Alice
    Munro.

    2 p.
    T.L.S. rejecting Simon's luck, relating
    reasons for rejection, and mentioning The
    beggar maid.

McGrath, Charles.   MsC 37.2.30.5
    Letter (1977 November 1), New York,
    N.Y., from C. McGrath, New Yorker, to
    Alice Munro, Clinton, Ont.

    1 p.
    T.L.S., with holograph postscript,
    rejecting Chaddeleys and Flemings, and
    relating reasons for rejection.

McGrath, Charles.   MsC 37.2.30.6
    Letter (1978 February 6), New York,
    N.Y., from C. McGrath, New Yorker, to
    Alice Munro, Clinton, Ont.

    1 p.
    T.L.S., with holograph annotation,
    enclosing galleys, probably for The
    moons of Jupiter, and suggesting minor
    revisions. Signed "Chip", probably
    Charles McGrath.

NIELSEN-FERNS INC.   MsC 37.2.31
    Letter (1977 January 4), Toronto, Ont., from
    W. Paterson Ferns, Nielsen-Ferns Inc., to Alice
    Munro, Clinton, Ont.

    1 item : 1 p.
    T.L.S. enclosing revised shooting script of
    screenplay (MsC 37.20.9) later titled 1847 : the
    Irish, part of television series The newcomers/Les
    arrivants. Letter explains revisions, and relates
    that A. Munro's screenplay will be shot in Summer
    1977.

NORTHWEST PASSAGE.   MsC 37.2.32
    Letter (197-), Bellingham, Wash., from Roxanne
    Park, Northwest Passage, to Alice Munro,
    Scarborough, Ont.

    1 item : 1 p.
    T.L.S. enclosing review of Lives of girls and
    women, and suggesting an interview for an article on
    A. Munro.

NOTRE DAME UNIVERSITY OF NELSON.   MsC 37.2.33
    Letters (1973 March 6-1973 May 4), from officials of
    Notre Dame University of Nelson to Alice Munro.

    3 items : 4 p.
    Letters concerning A. Munro's position as a sessional
    English instructor during 1973 summer school.

        Morey, Lorna A. D.   MsC 37.2.33.1
            Letter (1973 March 6), Nelson, B.C., from
            L. A. D. Morey, Chairman, English
            Department, Notre Dame University of
            Nelson, to Alice Munro, Victoria, B.C.

            1 p.
            T.L.S. discussing details related to
            A. Munro's summer school teaching position
            at Nelson. Mentions Thanks for the ride.

        Morey, Lorna A. D.   MsC 37.2.33.2
            Letter (1973 April 2), Nelson, B.C., from
            L. A. D. Morey, Chairman, English
            Department, Notre Dame University of
            Nelson, to Alice Munro, Victoria, B.C.

            2 p.
            T.L.S., with holograph annotation,
            relating information about English course
            to be taught by A. Munro at summer
            school.

Baravalle, E. D.   MsC 37.2.33.3
    Letter (1973 May 4), Nelson, B.C., from
    E. D. Baravalle, Director of Extension,
    Notre Dame University of Nelson, to Alice
    Munro, Victoria, B.C.

    1 p.
    T.L.S. discussing financial considerations
    related to summer school teaching position.

OBERON PRESS.   MsC 37.2.34
    Letter (1972 September 2), Ottawa, Ont., from
    Michael Macklem, Oberon Press, to Alice Munro.

    1 item : 1 p.
    T.L.S. requesting that Oberon Press be considered
    if A. Munro changes publishers.

ONTARIO. MINISTRY OF CULTURE AND RECREATION.
    HERITAGE CONSERVATION DIVISION.   MsC 37.2.35
    Letter (1978 April 18), Toronto, Ont., from Stephen
    A. Otto, Executive Director, Heritage Conservation
    Division, Ontario Ministry of Culture and Recreation,
    to Alice Munro, Clinton, Ont.

    1 item : 1 p.
    A.L.S. inquiring if A. Munro would be interested in
    writing descriptive articles to support preservation
    of historical buildings. Mentions Lives of girls and
    women and The newcomers/Les arrivants.

OXFORD UNIVERSITY PRESS.   MsC 37.2.36
    Letter (1962 July 23), Toronto, Ont., from Rosemary
    Duff, Promotion Manager, Oxford University Press,
    to Alice Munro, West Vancouver, B.C.

    1 item : 1 p.
    T.L.S. requesting photograph of A. Munro for
    inclusion in The first five years : a selection from
    the Tamarack Review. (Edited by Robert Weaver.
    Toronto: Oxford University Press, 1962.)

PACEY, DESMOND.   MsC 37.2.37
Letters (1961 July 6-1961 July 24), from D. Pacey to
Alice Munro.

2 items : 2 p.
Letters related to inclusion of Sunday afternoon in
anthology A book of Canadian stories.

Pacey, Desmond.   MsC 37.2.37.1
Letter (1961 July 6), Fredericton, N.B.,
from D. Pacey to Alice Munro, Toronto,
Ont.

1 p.
T.L.S. requesting permission to include
short story, possibly Sunday afternoon, in
A book of Canadian stories.

Pacey, Desmond.   MsC 37.2.37.2
Letter (1961 July 24), Fredericton, N.B.,
from D. Pacey to Alice Munro, Vancouver,
B.C.

1 p.
T.L.S. expressing appreciation for
biographical notes and for permission to
publish Sunday afternoon. Includes
A. Munro's unrelated holograph note on
the verso.

PLOUGHSHARES, INC.   MsC 37.2.38
Letter (1978(?) January 4), Cambridge, Mass., from
DeWitt Henry, Ploughshares, Inc., to Alice Munro.

1 item : 1 p.
T.L.S. discussing publication of Characters, and
suggesting minor revisions.

RYERSON PRESS.   MsC 37.2.39
    Letters (n.d., 1967 November 8-1970 March 4), from
    various Ryerson Press officials to Alice Munro.

    7 items : 11 p. on 10 leaves.
    Letters relating to publication of Dance of the happy
    shades, 1968 Governor General's Literary Award and
    television film of Postcard.

        Colombo, John Robert.   MsC 37.2.39.1
            Letter (n.d.), from J. R. Colombo,
            Assistant Editor, Ryerson Press, to Alice
            Munro, West Vancouver, B.C.

            1 p.
            T.L.S. relating to proposed collection of
            short stories, and suggesting possible
            inclusion of The Peace of Utrecht, The
            time of death, Sunday afternoon, Dance of
            the happy shades, The ounce of cure, also
            titled An ounce of cure, and The trip to
            the coast, also titled A trip to the coast.
            Dated as pre-1963 by A. Munro.

        Toppings, Earle.   MsC 37.2.39.2
            Letter (1967 November 8), from
            E. Toppings(?), Ryerson Press, to Alice
            Munro.

            1 p.
            T.L.S. enclosing copies of Postcard
            (MsC 37.6.39) and Walker Brothers cowboy
            (MsC 37.7.15) to be included in short
            story collection, probably Dance of the
            happy shades. Letter from "Earle",
            probably Earle Toppings.

        Ryerson Press.   MsC 37.2.39.3
            Royalty statement (1969 January 31),
            Toronto, Ont., from Ryerson Press to
            Alice Munro, Victoria, B.C.

            1 p.
            Typescript royalty statement for Dance of
            the happy shades for year ending
            January 31, 1969.

Farr, Robin.   MsC 37.2.39.4
    Letter (1969 March 18), Toronto, Ont.,
    from R. Farr, Editor-in-Chief, Ryerson
    Press, to Alice Munro, Victoria, B.C.

    1 p.
    T.L.S. enclosing advance copy of Canada
    Council press release listing leading
    nominees, including A. Munro for Dance of
    the happy shades, for 1968 Governor
    General's Literary Awards. Includes press
    release (1969 March 18), from Gerald
    Taaffe and Mario Lavoie, Canada Council.
    2 p. typescript; business card. 2 p. on
    1 leaf.

Coffin, Audrey.   MsC 37.2.39.5
    Letter (1969 April 24), Toronto, Ont.,
    from A. Coffin, Ryerson Press, to Alice
    Munro.

    1 p.
    A.L.S. congratulating A. Munro on
    winning award, probably Governor
    General's Literary Award. Mentions The
    Peace of Utrecht and Dance of the happy
    shades.

Truss, George A.   MsC 37.2.39.6
    Letter (1969 April 24), Toronto, Ont.,
    from G. A. Truss, Public Relations
    Manager, Ryerson Press, to Alice Munro,
    Victoria, B.C.

    1 p.
    T.L.S. making publicity arrangements for
    Toronto trip.

Coffin, Audrey.   MsC 37.2.39.7
    Letter (1970 March 4), Toronto, Ont.,
    from A. Coffin, Associate Editor, Ryerson
    Press, to Alice Munro, Victoria, B.C.

    1 p.
    T.L.S. discussing the Canadian
    Broadcasting Corporation television film of
    Postcard.

TORONTO LIFE.   MsC 37.2.40
    Letters (1977 September 23-1977 December 8), from
    Elizabeth Parr, Editor, Toronto Life, to Alice Munro.

    2 items : 2 p.
    Letters related to publication of Accident and Wild
    Swans.

        Parr, Elizabeth.   MsC 37.2.40.1
            Letter (1977 September 23), Toronto,
            Ont., from E. Parr, Senior Editor,
            Toronto Life, to Alice Munro, Victoria,
            B.C.

            1 p.
            T.L.S. enclosing galleys (MsC 37.13.28) of
            Accident, to be published in the November
            issue of Toronto Life.

        Parr, Elizabeth.   MsC 37.2.40.2
            Letter (1977 December 8), Toronto, Ont.,
            from E. Parr, Toronto Life, to Alice
            Munro, Clinton, Ont.

            1 p.
            T.L.S. enclosing galleys of Wild swans, to
            be published in Toronto Life. (Enclosed
            galleys possibly in MsC 37.12.20.)

TRENT UNIVERSITY.   MsC 37.2.41
    Letter (1973 December 3), Peterborough, Ont., from
    Michael Peterman, Department of English Literature,
    Trent University, to Alice Munro, London, Ont.

    1 item : 1 p.
    T.L.S. extending an invitation to participate in
    Trent University's weekend of Canadian Writers,
    honouring Margaret Laurence. Includes tentative
    schedule. 1 p. typescript (photocopy).

UNIVERSITY OF CALGARY.   MsC 37.2.42
    Letter (1977 October 7), Calgary, Alta., from
    Hallvard Dahlie, Head, Department of English,
    University of Calgary, to Alice Munro, Clinton, Ont.

    1 item : 1 p.
    T.L.S. discussing H. Dahlie's proposed essay for
    Ploughshares on A. Munro's fiction, and offering
    position as writer-in-residence at University of
    Calgary for 1978-1979.

UNIVERSITY OF REGINA.   MsC 37.2.43
    Letter (1976 February 11), Regina, Sask., from
    Lloyd H. Person, Head, Fine Arts and Humanities,
    University of Regina, to Alice Munro.

    1 item : 1 p.
    T.L.S. extending an invitation to participate in the
    "Canada '76" readings.

UNIVERSITY OF TORONTO.   MsC 37.2.44
    Letter (1977 January 17), Toronto, Ont., from Sam
    Solecki, Chairman, Committee for the Writer in
    Residence, University of Toronto, to Alice Munro,
    Clinton, Ont.

    1 item : 1 p.
    T.L.S. inquiring if A. Munro would be interested in
    the position of writer-in-residence for following
    year.

UNIVERSITY OF WESTERN ONTARIO.   MsC 37.2.45
    Letter (1976 February 12), London, Ont., from
    D. C. Williams, President and Vice-Chancellor,
    University of Western Ontario, to Alice Munro,
    Clinton, Ont.

    1 item : 1 p.
    T.L.S. requesting that A. Munro acccept the
    honourary degree of Doctor of Letters at spring
    convocation.

VAN BUREK, ANNE.   MsC 37.2.46
Letter (1975 March 17), Toronto, Ont., from A. Van
Burek to Alice Munro, Toronto, Ont.

1 item : 1 p.
T.L.S. inquiring about translating A. Munro's work
into French, and praising Lives of girls and women,
Dance of the happy shades and Something I've been
meaning to tell you.

VIRGINIA BARBER.   MsC 37.2.47
Letters (n.d., 1976 March 11-1978(?) January 5),
from, or forwarded by, Ginger Barber and Mary
Evans, of Virginia Barber, to Alice Munro.

22 items : 35 p. on 34 leaves.
Correspondence relating to periodical publication of
short stories, chiefly those later published in
collection Who do you think you are?. Includes
letters from editors and publishers forwarded by
Virginia Barber to A. Munro. Corporate name
changes to Virginia Barber Literary Agency, Inc.
toward the end of file.

      Barber, Ginger.   MsC 37.2.47.1
      Letter fragment (n.d.), from G. Barber,
      Literary Agent, Virginia Barber, to Alice
      Munro.

      1 p.
      Typescript signed letter fragment.
      Holograph annotations on verso.

      Barber, Ginger.   MsC 37.2.47.2
      Letter (1976 March 11), New York, N.Y.,
      from G. Barber, Literary Agent, Virginia
      Barber, to Alice Munro, Clinton, Ont.

      2 p.
      T.L.S. promoting Virginia Barber as a
      literary agency, and praising Material.

Barber, Ginger.   MsC 37.2.47.3
  Letter (1976 November 17), New York,
  N.Y., from G. Barber, Literary Agent,
  Virginia Barber, to Alice Munro, Clinton,
  Ont.

  1 p.
  T.L.S., with holograph postscript,
  discussing New Yorker interest in
  A. Munro's short stories and other
  business topics. Includes A. Munro's
  holograph annotation on verso.

New Yorker.   MsC 37.2.47.4
  Letter (1976 December 21), New York,
  N.Y., from Charles McGrath, New Yorker,
  to Ginger Barber, New York, N.Y.

  1 p.
  T.L.S. (photocopy) relating to publication
  of The beggar maid, and rejecting
  Accident and Pleistocene, later titled
  Characters. Includes G. Barber's
  holograph note to Alice Munro mentioning
  Accident and Providence.

Barber, Ginger.   MsC 37.2.47.5
  Letter (1977 January 20), from G. Barber,
  Literary Agent, Virginia Barber, to Alice
  Munro.

  1 p.
  T.L.S., with holograph postscript,
  discussing paperback rights for Dance of
  the happy shades and other copyright
  problems. Mentions Spelling and The red
  dress, also titled Red dress-1946.
  Encloses letter (1977 January 20), from
  G. Barber to Robin Brass, McGraw-Hill
  Ryerson Limited, Scarborough, Ont. 2 p.
  T.L.S. (carbon copy); letter (1977
  January 20), from G. Barber to Jack
  Stoddart, General Publishing Company,
  Toronto, Ont. 1 p. T.L.S. (carbon
  copy). Enclosed letters discuss paperback
  rights, and mention Something I've been
  meaning to tell you, as well as titles
  mentioned in covering letter.

Barber, Ginger.   MsC 37.2.47.6
     Letter (1977 March 2), New York, N.Y.,
     from G. Barber, Literary Agent, Virginia
     Barber, to Alice Munro.

     1 p.
     T.L.S. relating to publication of
     Providence, probably in Redbook, and
     discussing potential for publication in
     other periodicals. Encloses letter (1977
     February 28), New York, N.Y., from
     Charles McGrath, New Yorker, to
     G. Barber rejecting Mischief, and
     including G. Barber's holograph note to
     Alice Munro. 1 p. T.L.S.

Barber, Ginger.   MsC 37.2.47.7
     Letter (1977 March 14), from G. Barber,
     Literary Agent, Virginia Barber, to Alice
     Munro.

     1 p.
     T.L.S. enclosing cheque for publication of
     Providence in Redbook, and mentioning
     publication of Royal beatings in New
     Yorker and other topics. Includes
     holograph annotation on verso.

Barber, Ginger.   MsC 37.2.47.8
     Letter (1977 March 22), from G. Barber,
     Literary Agent, Virginia Barber, to Alice
     Munro.

     1 p.
     T.L.S. regarding permission granted to
     Oxford University Press to print excerpts
     of A. Munro's work. Encloses letter (1977
     March 8), New York, N.Y., from Kate
     Medina, Senior Editor, Doubleday, to
     Ginger Barber, Virginia Barber, New
     York, N.Y., praising Lives of girls and
     women, and expressing interest in
     publishing A. Munro's work. 1 p. T.L.S.
     (photocopy).

_____, Susan.   MsC 37.2.47.9
        Letter (1977 March 31), New York, N.Y.,
        from Susan _____, Virginia Barber, to
        Alice Munro.

        1 p.
        T.L.S. enclosing copy of Wild swans
        (MsC 37.12.18), and mentioning
        Grapefruit, probably Half a grapefruit.
        Includes letter (1977 March 22), Don Mills,
        Ont., from Martha Dzioba, Editorial
        Department, Oxford University Press, to
        Ginger Barber, Virginia Barber, New
        York, N.Y., regarding permission granted
        to publish excerpt from The colonel's hash
        resettled in Personal fictions : stories from
        Munro, Wiebe, Thomas and Blaise. 1 p.
        T.L.S. (photocopy).

Redbook.   MsC 37.2.47.10
        Letter (1977 April 6), New York, N.Y.,
        from Anne Mollegen Smith, Fiction Editor,
        Redbook, to Ginger Barber.

        2 p.
        T.L.S. (photocopy) suggesting revisions
        for Half a grapefruit.

Evans, Mary.   MsC 37.2.47.11
        Letter (1977 May 16), New York, N.Y.,
        from M. Evans, Virginia Barber, to Alice
        Munro, Clinton, Ont.

        1 p.
        T.L.S. regarding Gordon Lish's letter
        discussing possibilities and problems with
        Mischief. Includes letter (1977 May 13),
        New York, N.Y., from G. Lish, Esquire,
        to M. Evans. 2 p. on 1 leaf. T.L.S.

Evans, Mary.   MsC 37.2.47.12
    Letter (1977 June 13), New York, N.Y.,
    from M. Evans, Virginia Barber, to Alice
    Munro, Clinton, Ont.

    1 p.
    T.L.S. reporting that Cosmopolitan has
    rejected Accident, and enclosing
    manuscript (MsC 37.13.25).

Barber, Ginger.   MsC 37.2.47.13
    Letter (1977 June 15), from G. Barber,
    Literary Agent, Virginia Barber, to Alice
    Munro.

    2 p.
    T.L.S. relating that Ms. will publish The
    honeyman's daughter, published in Ms. as
    The honeyman's granddaughter, also titled
    Privilege. Also mentioning that Providence
    will be published in August Redbook and
    The beggar maid in a June New Yorker.

Barber, Ginger.   MsC 37.2.47.14
    Letter (1977 June 27), from G. Barber,
    Literary Agent, Virginia Barber, to Alice
    Munro.

    1 p.
    T.L.S. enclosing rough copy of New
    Yorker, probably including The beggar
    maid, and relating that Esquire has
    rejected Mischief.

Evans, Mary.   MsC 37.2.47.15
    Letter (1977 July 8), New York, N.Y.,
    from M. Evans, Virginia Barber, to Alice
    Munro, Clinton, Ont.

    1 p.
    T.L.S. enclosing letters. Includes letter
    (1977 July 4), Toronto, Ont., from John
    Pearce, Senior Editor, Clarke, Irwin and
    Company Limited, to Ginger Barber,
    Virginia Barber, New York, N.Y.,
    expressing enthusiasm for A. Munro's
    work. 1 p. T.L.S. (photocopy); letter
    (1977 July 7), New York, N.Y. from Alice
    _____, Alfred A. Knopf Incorporated, to
    Ginger Barber, praising The beggar maid.
    1 p. T.L.S. (photocopy).

Barber, Ginger.   MsC 37.2.47.16
    Letter (1977 August 16), from G. Barber,
    Literary Agent, Virginia Barber, to Alice
    Munro.

    1 p.
    T.L.S. enclosing cheque, and discussing
    submissions of Spelling, Mischief,
    Pleistocene, also titled Characters, and
    Wild swans to various periodicals.

Barber, Ginger.   MsC 37.2.47.17
    Letter (1977 September 15), from
    G. Barber, Literary Agent, Virginia
    Barber, to Lennart Sane, Lennart Sane
    Agency, Malmo, Sweden.

    1 p.
    T.L. (carbon copy) listing publishers to
    contact regarding rights for Dance of the
    happy shades, Lives of girls and women
    and Something I've been meaning to tell
    you.

Barber, Ginger.   MsC 37.2.47.18
    Letter (1977 October 7), New York, N.Y.,
    from G. Barber, Literary Agent, Virginia
    Barber, to Alice Munro.

    1 p.
    T.L.S. relating that Toronto Life will
    publish Wild swans, mentioning Pleistocene,
    later titled Characters, and discussing
    arrangement of a new collection, possibly
    to include Royal beatings, Privilege, Half a
    grapefruit, Wild swans, Spelling, Accident,
    The beggar maid, Mischief, Providence,
    Simon's luck and Mr. Black.

McGraw-Hill Ryerson Limited.   MsC 37.2.47.19
    Letter (1977 November 16), Scarborough,
    Ont., from Robin Brass, Managing Editor,
    McGraw-Hill Ryerson Limited, to Ginger
    Barber, of Virginia Barber, New York,
    N.Y.

    1 p.
    T.L.S. (photocopy) inquiring about
    publishing Alice Munro's new collection of
    short stories, probably Who do you think
    you are?. Includes G. Barber's holograph
    note to A. Munro.

Barber, Ginger.   MsC 37.2.47.20
    Letter (1977 November 21), from
    G. Barber, of Virginia Barber, to Linda
    McKnight, McClelland and Stewart Limited,
    Toronto, Ont.

    1 p.
    T.L. (carbon copy) discussing fees for
    Alice Munro's unidentified work, possibly
    A better place than home. Includes
    G. Barber's typescript note to A. Munro
    regarding copyright.

Evans, Mary.					MsC 37.2.47.21
	Letter (1978?), New York, N.Y., from
	M. Evans, Virginia Barber Literary
	Agency, Inc., to Alice Munro.

	1 p.
	A.L.S. relating that Viva will publish
	Emily, later revised and published as
	Simon's luck, and mentioning Mischief.

Ploughshares, Inc.					MsC 37.2.47.22
	Letter (1978(?) January 5), Cambridge,
	Mass., from DeWitt Henry, Ploughshares,
	Inc., to Ginger Barber.

	1 p.
	T.L.S. (photocopy) accepting Characters
	for publication, discussing other
	contributions to the issue, and inquiring if
	Alice Munro gives readings.

WATSON, PATRICK.					MsC 37.2.48
	Letter (1978 February 6), Carleton Place, Ont., from
	P. Watson to Alice Munro.

	1 item : 2 p.
	T.L.S. discussing possible television interview with
	A. Munro.

WEEKEND MAGAZINE.					MsC 37.2.49
	Letter (1978?), Toronto, Ont., from Judy _____,
	Weekend Magazine, to Alice Munro.

	1 item : 1 p.
	A.L.S. enclosing author's proof of Spelling
	(MsC 37.12.6).

WOMEN'S PRESS LTD.   MsC 37.2.50
    Letter (1977 September 5), London, England, from
    Stephanie Dowrick, Women's Press Ltd., to Alice
    Munro, New York, N.Y.

    1 item : 1 p.
    T.L.S. relating that A. Munro's book, probably
    Lives of girls and women, will be reprinted in
    paperback edition, and discussing other publishing
    topics.

WRITERS' UNION OF CANADA.   MsC 37.2.51
    Letters (n.d., 1973 March 6-1973 December 17), from
    Writers' Union of Canada officials, chiefly John
    Metcalf, to Alice Munro.

    3 items : 16 p.
    Letters relating chiefly to formation of the Writers'
    Union of Canada.

        Metcalf, John.   MsC 37.2.51.1
            Letter fragment (n.d.), from J. Metcalf,
            Writers' Union of Canada.

            1 p.
            Signed typescript (mimeograph) letter
            fragment related to formation of Writers'
            Union of Canada. Includes list of
            Canadian authors. 7 p. typescript
            (mimeograph).

        Metcalf, John.   MsC 37.2.51.2
            Letter (1973 March 6), Fredericton, N.B.,
            from J. Metcalf, Writers' Union of Canada,
            to Alice Munro.

            1 p.
            T.L.S. (photocopy) relating information
            about the proposed Writers' Union of
            Canada, and inviting A. Munro to join.

Writers' Union of Canada.
    Newsletter (1973 December 17), from
    Writers' Union of Canada.

    7 p.
    Typescript (photocopy) newsletter number
    five.

MsC 37.2.51.3

YORK UNIVERSITY.
    Letter (1974 January 18), Downsview, Ont., from
    D. R. Ewen, Chairman, Department of English, York
    University, to Alice Munro, London, Ont.

    1 item : 1 p.
    T.L.S. expressing regret over A. Munro's
    resignation as creative writing instructor.

MsC 37.2.52

YOUNG PEOPLE'S THEATRE CENTRE.
    Newsletter (1977 June 7), Toronto, Ont., from
    N. Gary Van Nest, Campaign Chairman, Young
    People's Theatre Centre.

    1 item : 2 p. on 1 leaf.
    Typescript (photocopy) newsletter discussing
    progress in construction of new theatre centre.

MsC 37.2.53

MUNRO, ALICE, 1931–
    Notes (197–, ca. 1976–1977).

    2 items : 2 p.
    Notes relating to financial matters.

MsC 37.2.54

Munro, Alice, 1931–
    Notes (197–).

    1 p.
    Holograph notes for agent relating to
    publishers' offers (per A. Munro).

MsC 37.2.54.1

Munro, Alice, 1931–   MsC 37.2.54.2
    Notes (ca. 1976–1977).

    1 p.
    Holograph notes related to income tax after
    publication of Something I've been meaning
    to tell you (per A. Munro).

MUNRO, ALICE, 1931–   MsC 37.2.55
    Letters (19-- December 5-1978 January 27), from
    readers to A. Munro.

    23 items : 29 p. on 27 leaves.
    Letters commending A. Munro's novel and short
    stories, and offering congratulations on winning the
    1968 Governor General's Literary Award and the
    Canada-Australia Literary Prize.   Letters arranged
    chronologically.

        Fitzhenry, Robert J.   MsC 37.2.55.1
            Letter (19-- December 5), from
            R. J. Fitzhenry to Alice Munro.

            1 p.
            A.L.S. commenting favourably on
            unidentified book by A. Munro.

        MacCallum, Russell.   MsC 37.2.55.2
            Letter (1965 May 30), Buckingham, P.Q.,
            from R. MacCallum to Alice Munro.

            1 p.
            T.L.S. praising The Peace of Utrecht and
            short story in Montrealer, probably Red
            dress-1946, and mentioning work
            R. MacCallum has had published.

Williams, Flo.   MsC 37.2.55.3
    Letter (1969 April 22), from F. and
    Bert Williams to Alice Munro.

    2 p. on 1 leaf.
    A.L.S. offering congratulations related to
    Dance of the happy shades, possibly for
    winning Governor General's Literary
    Award.

Bank Street P.T.A.   MsC 37.2.55.4
    Letter (1969 April 23), Victoria, B.C.,
    from Pamela Schwantje, Secretary, Bank
    Street P.T.A., to Alice Munro.

    1 p.
    T.L.S. offering congratulations on winning
    Governor General's Literary Award.

Mohart, Jean.   MsC 37.2.55.5
    Letter (1969 April 28), Vancouver, B.C.,
    from J. Mohart to Alice Munro, Victoria,
    B.C.

    1 p.
    T.L.S. offering congratulations, probably
    for Governor General's Literary Award,
    and enclosing newspaper clipping.

Waldman, Marcella.   MsC 37.2.55.6
    Letter (197-), from M. and Seymour
    Waldman to Alice Munro.

    1 p.
    A.L.S. commenting on A. Munro's books,
    and mentioning Lives of girls and women.

Hunter, Bob.   MsC 37.2.55.7
    Letter (1971 November 22), Toronto, Ont.,
    from B. Hunter to Alice Munro.

    3 p.
    A.L.S. praising Boys and girls and An
    ounce of cure.

MacLennan, Hugh.   MsC 37.2.55.8
    Letter (1973 January 18), from
    H. MacLennan to Alice Munro.

    1 p.
    T.L.S. commending A. Munro on
    unidentified television film presented by
    Canadian Broadcasting Corporation.

Keensworth, Barbara.   MsC 37.2.55.9
    Letter (1973 March 8), Pelham Manor,
    N.Y., from B. Keensworth to McCall's.

    1 p.
    A.L.S. expressing appreciation for
    publication of Red dress, also titled Red
    dress-1946.

Kreutzweiser, Erwin.   MsC 37.2.55.10
    Letter (1973 May 1), Ottawa, Ont., from
    E. Kreutzweiser to Alice Munro.

    1 p.
    T.L.S. praising Lives of girls and women.

Brown, Tamzin.   MsC 37.2.55.11
    Letter (1974 January 1), Hopkins, Minn.,
    from T. Brown to Alice Munro, Novato,
    Calif.

    1 p.
    A.L.S. expressing appreciation for Lives
    of girls and women, Dance of the happy
    shades and particularly Boys and girls.
    Includes envelope.

Walker, Johnny.   MsC 37.2.55.12
    Postcard (1974 September 4), North
    Vancouver, B.C., from J. Walker to Alice
    Munro, Scarborough, Ont.

    1 p.
    Holograph postcard commending A. Munro
    on Dance of the happy shades.

Koehler, Joyce.   MsC 37.2.55.13
    Letter (1974 December 1), Phoenix, Ariz.,
    from J. Koehler to Alice Munro.

    2 p. on 1 leaf.
    A.L.S. praising new collection of stories,
    probably Something I've been meaning to
    tell you, and expressing appreciation for
    Lives of girls and women and Dance of the
    happy shades.

Grosskopf, Myrna.   MsC 37.2.55.14
    Letter (1975 November 12), Seattle, Wash.,
    from M. Grosskopf to Alice Munro, New
    York, N.Y.

    2 p.
    T.L.S. expressing appreciation for
    A. Munro's books, mentioning Lives of
    girls and women, Dance of the happy
    shades, Something I've been meaning to
    tell you, An ounce of cure, Thanks for
    the ride, Forgiveness in families and The
    office.

Rafel, Ellen.   MsC 37.2.55.15
    Letter (1977?), New York, N.Y., from
    E. Rafel to Alice Munro.

    1 p.
    A.L.S. commending A. Munro for The
    beggar maid.

Kaplan, James.   MsC 37.2.55.16
    Letter (1977(?) June 23), from J. Kaplan
    to Alice Munro.

    1 p.
    T.L.S. praising The beggar maid.

Kellner, Mark A.   MsC 37.2.55.17
    Letter (1977 June 23), Rego Park, N.Y.,
    from M. A. Kellner to Alice Munro, New
    York, N.Y.

    1 p.
    T.L.S. expressing appreciation for The
    beggar maid.

Millar, Kenneth.   MsC 37.2.55.18
    Letter (1977 June 27), Santa Barbara,
    Calif., from K. Millar to Alice Munro.

    1 p.
    A.L.S. praising The beggar maid.

Morgan, Jeanne.   MsC 37.2.55.19
    Letter (1977 June 29), Los Angeles,
    Calif., from J. Morgan to Alice Munro.

    1 p.
    A.L.S. praising The beggar maid.

Maynard, Fredelle.   MsC 37.2.55.20
    Letter (1977 July 25), Durham, N.H., from
    F. Maynard to Alice Munro, Clinton, Ont.

    1 p.
    T.L.S. expressing appreciation for
    Something I've been meaning to tell you.
    Includes envelope.

Sradnick, Ellen.   MsC 37.2.55.21
    Letter (1977 October 11), New York,
    N.Y., from E. Sradnick to Alice Munro.

    1 p.
    A.L.S. commending Lives of girls and
    women, Red dress-1946, The beggar maid
    and Memorial.

Mallett, Jane.   MsC 37.2.55.22
    Letter (ca. 1977-1978), from J. Mallett to
    Alice Munro.

    1 p.
    A.L.S. offering congratulations on winning
    the Canada-Australia Literary Prize.

Copps, Bob.   MsC 37.2.55.23
    Letter (1978 January 27), Toronto, Ont.,
    from B. Copps to Alice Munro, New York,
    N.Y.

    2 p.
    T.L.S. praising Lives of girls and women.

MUNRO, ALICE, 1931–   MsC 37.3-5
NOVEL SERIES, CA. 1960-1978.

283 ITEMS.
CONSISTS OF UNPUBLISHED NOVEL WITH VARIANT
TITLES DEATH OF A WHITE FOX, THE NORWEGIAN AND
THE WHITE NORWEGIAN; AND NOVEL LIVES OF GIRLS
AND WOMEN, ORIGINALLY TITLED REAL LIFE.
MANUSCRIPT FRAGMENTS ONLY FOR THE UNPUBLISHED
NOVEL; FRAGMENTS UNDATED AND SORTED
ACCORDING TO STORY VERSION. INCLUDES
MANUSCRIPTS, FRAGMENTS AND REVIEWS FOR LIVES
OF GIRLS AND WOMEN; MANUSCRIPTS ARRANGED
ALPHABETICALLY BY CHAPTER TITLE, EARLY
FRAGMENTS WHICH APPEAR TO BE RELATED ARE
INCLUDED; MATERIAL UNDATED AND ROUGH SORTED
CHRONOLOGICALLY FOR EACH CHAPTER; COMPLETE
NOVEL MANUSCRIPTS AT END OF SERIES, FOLLOWED
BY CANADIAN, AMERICAN AND BRITISH REVIEWS.
MANUSCRIPT FRAGMENTS AND REVIEWS NOT ITEMIZED.

MUNRO, ALICE, 1931–   MsC 37.3.1
    Death of a white fox : novel fragments, 196-.

    5 items : 6 p.
    Untitled variant beginning fragments, possibly
    related to early versions of the unpublished novel
    Death of a white fox. Date established as 1960s by
    A. Munro. 1 p. holograph, 5 p. typescript.

MUNRO, ALICE, 1931–   MsC 37.3.2
    Death of a white fox : novel fragments, 196-.

    4 items : 9 p.
    Untitled typescript fragments, possibly from early
    versions of unpublished novel Death of a white
    fox. Date established as 1960s by A. Munro.

MUNRO, ALICE, 1931–   MsC 37.3.3
The white Norwegian, chapter I : novel, 196–.

2 items : 10 p.
Typescript fragments, tentatively identified as
from same draft. Probably early version of
unpublished novel, also sometimes titled Death of a
white fox. Date established as 1960s by A. Munro.

MUNRO, ALICE, 1931–   MsC 37.3.4
The Norwegian : novel, 196–.

1 item : 20 p. on 19 leaves.
Typescript with holograph revisions. Titled
fragment from unpublished novel, also sometimes
titled Death of a white fox. Date established as
1960s by A. Munro. Typescript fragment on verso
of last page.

MUNRO, ALICE, 1931–   MsC 37.3.5
Death of a white fox : novel fragments, 196–.

4 items : 15 p.
Typescript with holograph revisions. Untitled
fragments, possibly from more than one draft,
related to unpublished novel Death of a white
fox. Typescript fragments on verso of two pages.
Date established as 1960s by A. Munro.

MUNRO, ALICE, 1931–   MsC 37.3.6
The Norwegian, parts I-II : novel, 196–.

5 items : 32 p.
Typescript with holograph revisions. Titled
fragments from unpublished novel, also sometimes
called Death of a white fox. First four fragments
may be consecutive. Date established as 1960s by
A. Munro.

MUNRO, ALICE, 1931-   MsC 37.3.7
Death of a white fox, parts I-III : novel, 196-.

5 items : 50 p.
Typescript and typescript with holograph revisions.
Fragments may be consecutive. Date established as
1960s by A. Munro.

MUNRO, ALICE, 1931-   MsC 37.3.8
Death of a white fox : novel fragments, 196-.

2 items : 19 p.
Typescript and typescript with holograph
revisions. Holograph annotation on verso of one
page. Date established as 1960s by A. Munro.

MUNRO, ALICE, 1931-   MsC 37.3.9
Death of a white fox : novel fragments, 196-.

2 items : 27 p.
Typescript with holograph revisions. Fragments
possibly from same draft. Typescript fragments on
verso of three pages. Date established as 1960s by
A. Munro.

MUNRO, ALICE, 1931-   MsC 37.3.10
The Norwegian : novel fragments, 196-.

2 items : 9 p.
Typescript with holograph revisions. Fragments may
be consecutive. Includes holograph annotation "from
'The Norwegian'", also sometimes titled Death of a
white fox. Date established as 1960s by A. Munro.

MUNRO, ALICE, 1931–   MsC 37.3.11
   Death of a white fox : novel fragments, 196–.

   2 items : 7 p.
   Typescript. Variant ending fragments, second
   fragment labelled as part IV. Fragments may be
   from different drafts. Date established as 1960s by
   A. Munro.

MUNRO, ALICE, 1931–   MsC 37.3.12
   Lives of girls and women : Age of faith : novel
   fragments, n.d.

   3 items : 30 p.
   Holograph and typescript with holograph revisions.
   Fragments with sections related to Age of faith and
   Walker Brothers cowboy. 2 p. holograph, 28 p.
   typescript.

MUNRO, ALICE, 1931–   MsC 37.3.13
   Lives of girls and women : Age of faith : novel
   fragments, n.d.

   2 items : 2 p.
   Typescript fragments possibly related to Age of
   faith.

MUNRO, ALICE, 1931–   MsC 37.3.14
   Lives of girls and women : Age of faith : novel,
   n.d.

   1 item : 24 p.
   Typescript with holograph revisions.

MUNRO, ALICE, 1931–   MsC 37.4.1
   Lives of girls and women : Baptizing : novel
   fragments, n.d.

   8 items : 13 p.
   Typescript fragments with sections possibly related
   to Baptizing.

MUNRO, ALICE, 1931–   MsC 37.4.2
    Lives of girls and women : Baptizing : novel
    fragment, n.d.

    1 item : 9 p. on 8 leaves.
    Typescript fragment possibly related to early
    versions of Baptizing. Typescript fragment on verso
    of first page.

MUNRO, ALICE, 1931–   MsC 37.4.3
    Lives of girls and women : Baptizing : novel
    fragment, n.d.

    1 item : 20 p.
    Typescript with holograph revisions. Untitled
    ending fragment which includes A. Munro's
    holograph annotation on verso of last page: "Rough
    complete No. 6 Tone – too soggy G's character-
    point up, fiercer".

MUNRO, ALICE, 1931–   MsC 37.4.4
    Lives of girls and women : Baptizing : novel
    fragment, n.d.

    1 item : 5 p.
    Typescript with holograph revisions.

MUNRO, ALICE, 1931–   MsC 37.4.5
    Lives of girls and women : Baptizing : novel, n.d.

    1 item : 50 p. on 46 leaves.
    Typescript with holograph revisions. Includes
    A. Munro's annotations: "No. 6 semi-final" and
    "Changes: introspective con. Jerry, some inc. con
    Garnet, mother up when she gets home".

MUNRO, ALICE, 1931–   MsC 37.4.6
    Lives of girls and women : Baptizing : novel
    fragment, n.d.

    1 item : 20 p.
    Typescript with holograph revisions. Titled
    beginning fragment.

MUNRO, ALICE, 1931–   MsC 37.4.7
   Lives of girls and women : Baptizing : novel
   fragments, n.d.

   4 items : 6 p.
   Typescript fragments tentatively identified as being
   originally part of MsC 37.5.6.

MUNRO, ALICE, 1931–   MsC 37.4.8
   Lives of girls and women : Changes and
   ceremonies : novel fragments, n.d.

   8 items : 24 p.
   Typescript and typescript with holograph revisions.
   Fragments containing sections related to Changes and
   ceremonies. Fragment 3 titled I am the daughter of
   a river god; other fragments untitled.

MUNRO, ALICE, 1931–   MsC 37.4.9
   Lives of girls and women : Changes and
   ceremonies : novel fragments, n.d.

   6 items : 18 p. on 17 leaves.
   Holograph, typescript and typescript with holograph
   revisions. Untitled fragments with segments related
   to Changes and ceremonies. Fragment on verso of
   first page similar to beginning of I am the daughter
   of a river god. 1 p. holograph, 17 p. typescript.

MUNRO, ALICE, 1931–   MsC 37.4.10
   Lives of girls and women : Changes and
   ceremonies : novel fragment, n.d.

   1 item : 1 p.
   Typescript. Untitled fragment.

MUNRO, ALICE, 1931–   MsC 37.4.11
    Lives of girls and women : Changes and
    ceremonies : novel, n.d.

    1 item : 24 p.
    Typescript with holograph revisions. Titled.

MUNRO, ALICE, 1931–   MsC 37.4.12
    Lives of girls and women : Epilogue : the
    photographer : novel fragment, n.d.

    1 item : 1 p.
    Typescript. Untitled fragment.

MUNRO, ALICE, 1931–   MsC 37.4.13
    Lives of girls and women : Epilogue : the
    photographer : novel, n.d.

    1 item : 10 p.
    Typescript with holograph revisions. Untitled.

MUNRO, ALICE, 1931–   MsC 37.4.14
    Lives of girls and women : Epilogue : the
    photographer : novel fragment, n.d.

    1 item : 3 p.
    Typescript. Ending fragment.

MUNRO, ALICE, 1931–   MsC 37.4.15
    Lives of girls and women : Epilogue : the
    photographer : novel, n.d.

    2 items : 11 p.
    Typescript with holograph revisions. Fragments
    possibly consecutive. Title "Death of Caroline"
    stroked out.

MUNRO, ALICE, 1931–   MsC 37.4.16
    Lives of girls and women : Epilogue : the
    photographer : novel fragments, n.d.

    4 items : 5 p.
    Typescript and typescript with holograph revisions.
    Variant ending fragments.

MUNRO, ALICE, 1931–   MsC 37.4.17
    Lives of girls and women : Epilogue : the
    photographer : novel, 1971 January 24.

    1 item : 9 p.
    Typescript. Untitled.

MUNRO, ALICE, 1931–   MsC 37.4.18
    Lives of girls and women : The Flats Road : novel
    fragments, n.d.

    4 items : 7 p. on 6 leaves.
    Holograph and typescript fragments, possibly
    related to early versions of The Flats Road.   3 p.
    holograph, 4 p. typescript.

MUNRO, ALICE, 1931–   MsC 37.4.19
    Lives of girls and women : The Flats Road : novel,
    n.d.

    1 item : 24 p.
    Typescript. Untitled.

MUNRO, ALICE, 1931–   MsC 37.4.20
    Lives of girls and women : The Flats Road : novel,
    n.d.

    3 items : 30 p.
    Typescript and typescript with holograph revisions.
    Items 2 and 3 are variant endings, probably
    continuations of item 1.

MUNRO, ALICE, 1931–   MsC 37.4.21
    Lives of girls and women : Heirs of the living
    body : novel fragments, n.d.

    26 items : 50 p. on 49 leaves.
    Typescript and typescript with holograph revisions.
    Untitled fragments about the "Musgrave house",
    sometimes called the "MacQuarrie" or "Halloway
    house". Fragments related to early versions of
    Heirs of the living body. One fragment titled
    Seasons in Tuppertown.

MUNRO, ALICE, 1931–   MsC 37.4.22
    Lives of girls and women : Heirs of the living
    body : novel fragments, n.d.

    12 items : 42 p. on 41 leaves.
    Holograph, typescript and typescript with holograph
    revisions. Untitled fragments chiefly about the
    "Musgrave house". Elements of some fragments
    similar to sections in Heirs of the living body.
    2 p. holograph, 40 p. typescript.

MUNRO, ALICE, 1931–   MsC 37.4.23
    Lives of girls and women : Heirs of the living
    body : novel fragments, n.d.

    4 items : 16 p.
    Typescript and typescript with holograph revisions.
    Untitled fragments with sections related to Heirs of
    the living body. Fragments may be from more than
    one draft.

MUNRO, ALICE, 1931–   MsC 37.4.24
    Lives of girls and women : Heirs of the living
    body : novel fragments, n.d.

    4 items : 14 p.
    Typescript with holograph revisions. Titled
    beginning fragment. Fragments possibly from one
    draft.

MUNRO, ALICE, 1931–   MsC 37.4.25
    Lives of girls and women : Family funeral : novel,
    n.d.

    1 item : 20 p.
    Typescript with holograph revisions. Early version
    of chapter later titled Heirs of the living body.
    Annotation on verso of MsC 37.4.25.f3 "Roughed for
    No 7".

MUNRO, ALICE, 1931–   MsC 37.4.26
    Lives of girls and women : Heirs of the living
    body : novel, n.d.

    1 item : 16 p.
    Typescript with holograph revisions. Untitled.

MUNRO, ALICE, 1931–   MsC 37.4.27
    Lives of girls and women : Heirs of the living
    body : novel, n.d.

    1 item : 27 p. on 26 leaves.
    Typescript with holograph fragment on verso of last
    page. Titled.

MUNRO, ALICE, 1931–   MsC 37.4.28
    Lives of girls and women : Heirs of the living
    body : novel fragments, n.d.

    11 items : 36 p.
    Typescript and typescript with holograph revisions.
    Titled. Fragments probably from one draft; includes
    several variant pages.

MUNRO, ALICE, 1931–   MsC 37.4.29
    Lives of girls and women : Lives of girls and
    women : novel fragment, n.d.

    1 item : 2 p.
    Typescript with holograph revisions. Untitled
    fragment possibly related to early versions of Lives
    of girls and women.

MUNRO, ALICE, 1931–   MsC 37.4.30
   Lives of girls and women : Lives of girls and
   women : novel fragment, n.d.

   1 item : 6 p.
   Typescript with holograph revisions. Untitled
   fragment with sections related to Lives of girls and
   women and Princess Ida.

MUNRO, ALICE, 1931–   MsC 37.4.31
   Lives of girls and women : Lives of girls and
   women : novel, n.d.

   2 items : 32 p.
   Typescript with holograph revisions. Titled.
   Fragments probably consecutive. Appears to be
   complete.

MUNRO, ALICE, 1931–   MsC 37.4.32
   Lives of girls and women : Lives of girls and
   women : novel fragment, n.d.

   1 item : 5 p.
   Typescript with holograph revisions. Ending
   fragment, possibly original ending for MsC 37.4.33.

MUNRO, ALICE, 1931–   MsC 37.4.33
   Lives of girls and women : Lives of girls and
   women : novel, n.d.

   1 item : 34 p.
   Typescript with holograph revisions. Titled.

MUNRO, ALICE, 1931–   MsC 37.4.34
   Lives of girls and women : Princess Ida : novel
   fragments, n.d.

   6 items : 8 p. on 7 leaves.
   Holograph and typescript. Untitled fragments, most
   beginning "My mother sold encyclopedias". Possibly
   related to early versions of Princess Ida. 2 p.
   holograph, 6 p. typescript.

MUNRO, ALICE, 1931–   MsC 37.4.35
    Lives of girls and women : Princess Ida : novel
    fragments, n.d.

    2 items : 3 p.
    Typescript untitled fragments possibly related to
    early versions of Princess Ida.

MUNRO, ALICE, 1931–   MsC 37.4.36
    Lives of girls and women : Princess Ida : novel,
    n.d.

    1 item : 18 p.
    Typescript with holograph revisions. Untitled.
    Version similar to MsC 37.5.2, identified by Alice
    Munro as part of the "conventional novel".

MUNRO, ALICE, 1931–   MsC 37.4.37
    Lives of girls and women : Princess Ida : novel
    fragments, n.d.

    2 items : 14 p.
    Typescript with holograph revisions. Untitled
    fragments, possibly from one draft; similar version
    to MsC 37.4.36.

MUNRO, ALICE, 1931–   MsC 37.4.38
    Lives of girls and women : Princess Ida : novel
    fragments, n.d.

    2 items : 13 p.
    Typescript with holograph revisions. First fragment
    titled; fragments possibly from one draft.

MUNRO, ALICE, 1931–   MsC 37.4.39
    Lives of girls and women : Princess Ida : novel
    fragments, n.d.

    2 items : 2 p.
    Typescript and typescript with holograph revisions.
    Titled first page and ending.

MUNRO, ALICE, 1931–   MsC 37.4.40
    Lives of girls and women : novel fragments, n.d.

    2 items : 5 p.
    Typescript and typescript with holograph revisions.
    Untitled fragments from unidentified chapter(s).

MUNRO, ALICE, 1931–   MsC 37.4.41
    Lives of girls and women, parts 1-8 : novel, n.d.

    1 item : 67 p.
    Typescript with holograph revisions. Untitled.
    Identified by A. Munro as part of the "more
    conventional novel" version, later put into "cyclets".
    Page 21 missing. Elements of part 8 similar to short
    story The found boat.

MUNRO, ALICE, 1931–   MsC 37.5.1
    Lives of girls and women, part 12 : novel, n.d.

    1 item : 10 p.
    Typescript with holograph revisions. Identified
    by A. Munro as part of the "more conventional
    novel" version, later put into "cyclets". Related to
    Princess Ida in the published version.

MUNRO, ALICE, 1931–   MsC 37.5.2
    Lives of girls and women, part 3 : novel, n.d.

    1 item : 19 p.
    Typescript with holograph revisions. Identified
    by A. Munro as part of the "more conventional
    novel" version, later put into "cyclets". Similar
    to MsC 37.4.36 and to parts of Princess Ida in
    published version.

MUNRO, ALICE, 1931–   MsC 37.5.3
    Lives of girls and women : novel fragment, n.d.

    1 item : 20 p.
    Typescript with holograph revisions. Fragment
    identified by A. Munro as part of the "more
    conventional novel" version, later put into "cyclets".
    Related to Changes and ceremonies in published
    version.

MUNRO, ALICE, 1931–   MsC 37.5.4
    Lives of girls and women : novel fragment, n.d.

    1 item : 1 p.
    Typescript with holograph revision. Fragment
    identified by A. Munro as part of the "more
    conventional novel" version, later put into "cyclets".

MUNRO, ALICE, 1931–   MsC 37.5.5
    Lives of girls and women : Death of Caroline : novel
    fragments, n.d.

    2 items : 10 p.
    Typescript with holograph revisions. First fragment
    titled. Fragments identified by A. Munro as part of
    the "conventional novel" version, later put into
    "cyclets". Title Marion & Caroline : Uncle Craig &
    me stroked out. Related to Epilogue : the
    photographer and Heirs of the living body in the
    published version.

MUNRO, ALICE, 1931–   MsC 37.5.6
    Real life : novel, n.d.

    1 item : 221 p.
    Typescript with holograph revisions. Published as
    Lives of girls and women. Lacks final chapter of
    published version. According to A. Munro
    consideration was given to publishing the novel
    without Epilogue : the photographer.

MUNRO, ALICE, 1931–   MsC 37.5.7-9
    Real life : novel, n.d.

    1 item : 78 p. on 75 leaves ; 70 p. ; 59 p.
    Typescript (carbon copy) with holograph additions
    and revisions; p. 58 typescript; p. 55 missing.
    Majority of text is copy of MsC 37.5.10-11 before
    revisions and with variant ending. Title page
    includes Alice Munro's signature and holograph
    annotation "This manuscript is in seven sections – all
    titled – with a short, untitled, Roman-numeralled
    section at the end. A.M.". Published as Lives of
    girls and women.

MUNRO, ALICE, 1931–   MsC 37.5.10-11
    Lives of girls and women : novel, n.d.

    1 item : 94 p. ; 116 p.
    Typescript with holograph revisions; holograph title
    page; p. 58 typescript (carbon copy). Pages 30-31
    missing. Copy edited for publisher.

MUNRO, ALICE, 1931–   MsC 37.5.12
    Lives of girls and women : novel fragments, n.d.

    4 items : 5 p.
    Typescript. Pages 22, 51, 115, 186-187; probably
    originally part of MsC 37.5.10-11. Three pages
    crossed out.

MUNRO, ALICE, 1931–   MsC 37.5.13
    Lives of girls and women : novel fragment, n.d.

    1 item : 3 p.
    Typescript. Pages 186-187A; probably a preliminary
    revision from MsC 37.5.10-11.

MUNRO, ALICE, 1931–   MsC 37.5.14
    Lives of girls and women : Canadian reviews,
    1971 October 30–1978 July.

    25 items : 31 p.
    Newsclippings and photocopies of reviews from
    newspapers and periodicals published in Canada.
    Arranged chronologically.

MUNRO, ALICE, 1931–   MsC 37.5.15
    Lives of girls and women : American reviews,
    1972 July 31–1974 April.

    55 items : 83 p.
    Newsclippings and photocopies of reviews from
    newspapers and periodicals published in the United
    States. Includes one radio review. Arranged
    chronologically.

MUNRO, ALICE, 1931–   MsC 37.5.16
    Lives of girls and women : British reviews, n.d.,
    1973 October 20–1978 March 17.

    13 items : 15 p.
    Newsclippings and photocopies of reviews from
    newspapers and periodicals published in Great
    Britain. Arranged chronologically.

MUNRO, ALICE, 1931–   MsC 37.5.17
    Lives of girls and women : promotional material,
    n.d.

    1 item : oversize.
    Poster advertising McGraw-Hill Ryerson edition of
    Lives of girls and women.

MUNRO, ALICE, 1931–   Msc 37.6.1–
COLLECTED SHORT STORY SERIES, CA. 1950-1978.   37.14.14

747 ITEMS.
CONSISTS OF SHORT STORY COLLECTIONS DANCE OF
THE HAPPY SHADES, SOMETHING I'VE BEEN MEANING
TO TELL YOU, WHO DO YOU THINK YOU ARE? AND THE
MOONS OF JUPITER. SHORT STORY COLLECTIONS
ARRANGED CHRONOLOGICALLY BY DATE OF
PUBLICATION. SHORT STORY MANUSCRIPTS
ARRANGED ALPHABETICALLY BY TITLE WITHIN EACH
COLLECTION; EARLY APPARENTLY RELATED
FRAGMENTS INCLUDED. MATERIAL ROUGH SORTED
CHRONOLOGICALLY FOR EACH TITLE. MANUSCRIPTS
FOR THREE SHORT STORIES ONLY FROM THE MOONS
OF JUPITER. COLLECTION MANUSCRIPTS FOR
SOMETHING I'VE BEEN MEANING TO TELL YOU AND
WHO DO YOU THINK YOU ARE? ARE FILED AT END OF
RESPECTIVE COLLECTIONS. MANUSCRIPTS ARE
FOLLOWED BY REVIEWS IN ALL COLLECTIONS EXCEPT
THE MOONS OF JUPITER. REVIEWS FOR THREE
ANTHOLOGIES WHICH INCLUDE SHORT STORIES FROM
DANCE OF THE HAPPY SHADES ARE FILED AFTER
REVIEWS FOR THAT COLLECTION.

MUNRO, ALICE, 1931–   Msc 37.6.1
     Dance of the happy shades : Boys and girls : short
     story fragments, n.d.

     5 items : 8 p.
     Typescript fragments possibly related to early
     versions of Boys and girls.

MUNRO, ALICE, 1931–   Msc 37.6.2
     Dance of the happy shades : Boys and girls : short
     story fragment, n.d.

     1 item : 5 p. on 4 leaves.
     Holograph and typescript. Titled fragment.   3 p.
     holograph, 2 p. typescript.

MUNRO, ALICE, 1931–   MsC 37.6.3
Dance of the happy shades : Boys and girls : short
story fragment, n.d.

1 item : 3 p.
Typescript. Titled fragment.

MUNRO, ALICE, 1931–   MsC 37.6.4
Dance of the happy shades : Boys and girls : short
story fragments, n.d.

3 items : 10 p. on 9 leaves.
Typescript. Untitled fragments, possibly
consecutive.

MUNRO, ALICE, 1931–   MsC 37.6.5
Dance of the happy shades : Boys and girls : short
story fragment, n.d.

1 item : 5 p.
Typescript with holograph revisions. Titled
fragment.

MUNRO, ALICE, 1931–   MsC 37.6.6
Dance of the happy shades : Boys and girls : short
story, n.d.

1 item : 15 p.
Typescript. Titled.

MUNRO, ALICE, 1931–   MsC 37.6.7
Dance of the happy shades : Boys and girls : short
story, n.d.

1 item : 17 p. on 16 leaves.
Typescript. Titled.

MUNRO, ALICE, 1931–   MsC 37.6.8
    Dance of the happy shades : Dance of the happy
    shades : short story, ca. 1960-1961.

    1 item : 14 p.
    Typescript with holograph corrections. Titled The
    dance of the happy shades. Signed "Alice Munro".
    Includes holograph annotation "CBC Sunday night–
    October 30th". Identified by A. Munro as
    ca. 1960-1961 and as having been broadcast by CBC
    before being sold to the Montrealer.

MUNRO, ALICE, 1931–   MsC 37.6.9
    Dance of the happy shades : Dance of the happy
    shades : short story fragment, n.d.

    1 item : 1 p.
    Typescript. Ending fragment.

MUNRO, ALICE, 1931–   MsC 37.6.10
    Dance of the happy shades.
    p. 5, 22-26.

    Detached from the Montrealer, v. 35, no. 2,
    February 1961.

MUNRO, ALICE, 1931–   MsC 37.6.11
    Good-by Myra.
    p. 1, 16-17, 55-58.

    Detached from Chatelaine, v. 28, no. 7, July 1956.
    Includes deletions and holograph revisions. Later
    published as Day of the butterfly in short story
    collection Dance of the happy shades.

MUNRO, ALICE, 1931-   MsC 37.6.12
    Day of the butterfly : page proofs, 1973.
    p. 241-244, 246-249, 251-253, 255-257.

    Typescript (photocopy) page proofs for Canadian
    edition of the elementary school language series The
    world of language, published by McGraw-Hill
    Ryerson Limited. Includes repository photocopy of
    covering letter (original MsC 37.2.25.3) requesting
    permission to delete marked passages.

MUNRO, ALICE, 1931-   MsC 37.6.13
    Dance of the happy shades : Images : short story
    fragments, n.d.

    11 items : 12 p. on 11 leaves.
    Typescript. Fragments about "the storm porch",
    possibly related to early versions of Images.

MUNRO, ALICE, 1931-   MsC 37.6.14
    Dance of the happy shades : Visiting : short story
    fragment, n.d.

    1 item : 1 p.
    Typescript. Titled fragment with segments similar to
    early versions of Images.

MUNRO, ALICE, 1931-   MsC 37.6.15
    Dance of the happy shades : Images : short story
    fragments, n.d.

    11 items : 31 p. on 26 leaves.
    Typescript and holograph. Fragments of various
    early versions about "the storm porch" and/or "Mary
    MacQuarrie". The versos of several pages contain
    unrelated holograph poems. 5 p. holograph, 26 p.
    typescript.

MUNRO, ALICE, 1931-   MsC 37.6.16
   Dance of the happy shades : Images : short story
   fragments, n.d.

   12 items : 35 p. on 34 leaves.
   Holograph, typescript and typescript with holograph
   revisions. Fragments about "the trapline" from
   various early versions. 6 p. holograph, 28 p.
   typescript.

MUNRO, ALICE, 1931-   MsC 37.6.17
   Dance of the happy shades : Images : short story
   fragments, n.d.

   4 items : 17 p. on 15 leaves.
   Typescript and typescript with holograph revisions.
   Fragments 1 and 2 possibly from same draft;
   fragments 3 and 4 are variant endings. Text on
   verso of fragment 1 is not sequential, but possibly
   part of same draft.

MUNRO, ALICE, 1931-   MsC 37.6.18
   Dance of the happy shades : The landlord : short
   story fragment, n.d.

   1 item : 5 p.
   Typescript with holograph revisions. Titled. Later
   published as The office. Possibly from same draft
   as MsC 37.6.19.

MUNRO, ALICE, 1931-   MsC 37.6.19
   Dance of the happy shades : The office : short
   story fragment, n.d.

   1 item : 9 p.
   Typescript. Untitled. Fragment possibly
   consecutive to preceding fragment (MsC 37.6.18).

MUNRO, ALICE, 1931–   MsC 37.6.20
Dance of the happy shades : The office : short
story, n.d.

1 item : 16 p.
Typescript. Signed "Alice Munro". Includes
annotation "Dear Earle – Here it is in manuscript – I
lost the magazine" (probably to Earle Toppings at
Ryerson Press). Holograph annotation of Vancouver
address stroked out.

MUNRO, ALICE, 1931–   MsC 37.6.21
Dance of the happy shades : An ounce of
cure : short story, n.d.

1 item : 14 p.
Typescript. Titled The ounce of cure; also
published as An ounce of cure. Signed
"Alice Munro".

MUNRO, ALICE, 1931–   MsC 37.6.22
Dance of the happy shades : An ounce of
cure : short story, n.d.

1 item : 14 p.
Typescript. Titled The ounce of cure, revised to
An ounce of cure. Signature "Alice Munro" stroked
out. Copy edited for unidentified publisher.

MUNRO, ALICE, 1931–   MsC 37.6.23
Dance of the happy shades : An ounce of
cure : short story, n.d.

1 item : 11 p.
Typescript. Untitled.

MUNRO, ALICE, 1931–   MsC 37.6.24
Dance of the happy shades : An ounce of
cure : short story, n.d.

1 item : 11 p.
Typescript with holograph revisions. Titled Some
ounces of cure; published as An ounce of cure.
Signed "Alice Munro".

MUNRO, ALICE, 1931–   MsC 37.6.25
    Dance of the happy shades : Places at home : title
    page, n.d.

    1 item : 1 p.
    Typescript. Signed "Alice Munro". Later published
    as The Peace of Utrecht.

MUNRO, ALICE, 1931–   MsC 37.6.26
    Dance of the happy shades : Places at home : short
    story fragment, n.d.

    1 item : 7 p.
    Typescript with holograph revisions. Titled. Later
    published as The Peace of Utrecht.

MUNRO, ALICE, 1931–   MsC 37.6.27
    Dance of the happy shades : The Peace of
    Utrecht : short story fragments, n.d.

    2 items : 9 p.
    Typescript. First fragment titled. Second fragment
    similar to p. 5 of first fragment.

MUNRO, ALICE, 1931–   MsC 37.6.28
    Dance of the happy shades : The Peace of
    Utrecht : short story fragment, n.d.

    1 item : 6 p.
    Typescript. Untitled beginning fragment.

MUNRO, ALICE, 1931–   MsC 37.6.29
    Dance of the happy shades : The Peace of
    Utrecht : short story fragment, n.d.

    1 item : 1 p.
    Typescript.

MUNRO, ALICE, 1931–   MsC 37.6.30
    Dance of the happy shades : The Peace of
    Utrecht : short story fragment, n.d.

    1 item : 12 p.
    Typescript. Ending fragment.

MUNRO, ALICE, 1931–   MsC 37.6.31
    Dance of the happy shades : The Peace of
    Utrecht : short story fragment, n.d.

    1 item : 4 p.
    Typescript.

MUNRO, ALICE, 1931–   MsC 37.6.32
    Dance of the happy shades : The Peace of
    Utrecht : short story fragment, n.d.

    1 item : 2 p.
    Typescript. Ending fragment.

MUNRO, ALICE, 1931–   MsC 37.6.33
    Dance of the happy shades : The distant scene,
    parts II-III : short story fragments, n.d.

    3 items : 9 p.
    Typescript. First fragment titled The distant scene,
    part II; part III incomplete. Later published as The
    Peace of Utrecht. Fragments possibly consecutive.

MUNRO, ALICE, 1931–   MsC 37.6.34
    Dance of the happy shades : The Peace of
    Utrecht : short story fragments, n.d.

    2 items : 2 p.
    Typescript.

MUNRO, ALICE, 1931–   MsC 37.6.35
     Dance of the happy shades : The Peace of
     Utrecht : short story fragment, n.d.

     1 item : 3 p.
     Typescript.   Paginated ending fragment.

MUNRO, ALICE, 1931–   MsC 37.6.36
     The Peace of Utrecht.
     p. 5-21.

     In Tamarack Review, no. 15, Spring 1960.   Also
     includes duplicate copy of published short story
     detached from Tamarack Review.

MUNRO, ALICE, 1931–   MsC 37.6.37
     Dance of the happy shades : Postcard : short story
     fragment, n.d.

     1 item : 4 p.
     Typescript.

MUNRO, ALICE, 1931–   MsC 37.6.38
     Dance of the happy shades : Postcard : short story,
     n.d.

     1 item : 16 p.
     Typescript with holograph revisions.   Untitled.

MUNRO, ALICE, 1931–   MsC 37.6.39
     Dance of the happy shades : Postcard : short story,
     1967.

     1 item : 17 p.
     Typescript (photocopy).   Titled.   Signed
     "Alice Munro".   Includes repository photocopy of
     covering letter (original MsC 37.2.39.2) from
     Earle Toppings, Ryerson Press, accepting Postcard
     for short story collection, probably Dance of the
     happy shades.

MUNRO, ALICE, 1931-   MsC 37.6.40
    Postcard : newsclipping, 1970 September 26.

    1 item : 1 p.
    Newspaper photograph from the Victoria Daily Times
    of a scene from Canadian Broadcasting Corporation
    television production of Postcard shown on Theatre
    Canada.

MUNRO, ALICE, 1931-   MsC 37.6.41
    Dance of the happy shades : Red dress-1946 : short
    story fragments, n.d.

    2 items : 2 p.
    Typescript. Fragments possibly related to early
    versions of Red dress-1946.

MUNRO, ALICE, 1931-   MsC 37.6.42
    Dance of the happy shades : Red dress-1946 : short
    story fragments, n.d.

    2 items : 5 p.
    Typescript and typescript with holograph revisions.
    Untitled fragments possibly from same early draft.

MUNRO, ALICE, 1931-   MsC 37.6.43
    Dance of the happy shades : Red dress-1946 : short
    story fragments, n.d.

    6 items : 17 p. on 16 leaves.
    Typescript and typescript with holograph revisions.
    First two fragments titled A red dress, 1946.

MUNRO, ALICE, 1931-   MsC 37.6.44
    Dance of the happy shades : Red dress-1946 : short
    story, n.d.

    1 item : 14 p. on 12 leaves.
    Typescript with holograph revisions. Titled A red
    dress, 1946. Unrelated fragment on verso of one
    page.

MUNRO, ALICE, 1931–   MsC 37.6.45
   Red dress–1946.
   p. 28–34.

   In the Montrealer, v. 39, no. 5, May 1965.

MUNRO, ALICE, 1931–   MsC 37.6.46
   Dance of the happy shades : Suburban story : short
   story, n.d.

   1 item : 10 p.
   Typescript. Published as The shining houses.
   Pages damaged in upper right corners, missing part
   of text.

MUNRO, ALICE, 1931–   MsC 37.6.47
   Dance of the happy shades : The shining
   houses : short story, n.d.

   1 item : 15 p.
   Typescript with holograph revisions. Titled.
   Signed "Alice Munro".

MUNRO, ALICE, 1931–   MsC 37.6.48
   Dance of the happy shades : The shining
   houses : short story fragment, n.d.

   1 item : 6 p.
   Typescript with holograph additions and revisions.

MUNRO, ALICE, 1931–   MsC 37.6.49
   Dance of the happy shades : The shining
   houses : short story, n.d.

   1 item : 12 p.
   Typescript (carbon copy) with copy editing. Titled.
   Title page includes typescript annotation "by Alice
   Munro", with a stroked out Vancouver address.

MUNRO, ALICE, 1931-   MsC 37.6.50
Dance of the happy shades : The shining
houses : short story fragment, n.d.

1 item : 1 p.
Typescript with copy editing. Variant ending
fragment, possibly replacing p. 11-12 in
MsC 37.6.49.

MUNRO, ALICE, 1931-   MsC 37.6.51
Dance of the happy shades : Sunday
afternoon : short story fragment, n.d.

1 item : 6 p.
Untitled holograph fragment with sections possibly
related to early versions of Sunday afternoon and
The beggar maid.

MUNRO, ALICE, 1931-   MsC 37.6.52
Dance of the happy shades : Sunday
afternoon : short story fragment, n.d.

1 item : 3 p.
Untitled typescript fragment with sections possibly
related to Sunday afternoon and The beggar maid.

MUNRO, ALICE, 1931-   MsC 37.6.53
Dance of the happy shades : Sunday
afternoon : short story fragments, n.d.

2 items : 2 p.
Typescript. Untitled fragments, possibly related to
early versions of Sunday afternoon.

MUNRO, ALICE, 1931-   MsC 37.6.54
Dance of the happy shades : Sunday
afternoon : short story fragments, n.d.

2 items : 2 p.
Typescript. Untitled fragments, possibly related to
early versions of Sunday afternoon.

MUNRO, ALICE, 1931–   MsC 37.6.55
    Dance of the happy shades : Sunday
    afternoon : short story fragment, n.d.

    1 item : 3 p. on 2 leaves.
    Holograph. Untitled fragment, possibly related to
    early versions of Sunday afternoon.

MUNRO, ALICE, 1931–   MsC 37.6.56
    Dance of the happy shades : Sunday
    afternoon : short story fragments, n.d.

    4 items : 4 p.
    Typescript. Untitled fragments, possibly related to
    early versions of Sunday afternoon.

MUNRO, ALICE, 1931–   MsC 37.6.57
    Dance of the happy shades : Sunday
    afternoon : short story fragment, n.d.

    1 item : 8 p.
    Typescript. Untitled fragment, possibly related to
    early versions of Sunday afternoon.

MUNRO, ALICE, 1931–   MsC 37.6.58
    Dance of the happy shades : Sunday
    afternoon : short story, n.d.

    1 item : 13 p.
    Typescript with holograph revisions. Originally
    titled The temporary position, revised to Sunday
    afternoon.

MUNRO, ALICE, 1931–   MsC 37.6.59
    Dance of the happy shades : Sunday
    afternoon : short story, n.d.

    1 item : 14 p.
    Typescript with holograph corrections. Titled.

MUNRO, ALICE, 1931–   Msc 37.6.60
Dance of the happy shades : Thanks for the
ride : short story fragments, n.d.

3 items : 9 p.
Typescript. First fragment titled. Signed "Alice
Laidlaw", maiden name of A. Munro. Fragments
probably part of one draft; missing p. 4–6, 12 and
ending. Page 1 damaged, missing part of text.

MUNRO, ALICE, 1931–   Msc 37.6.61
Dance of the happy shades : Thanks for the
ride : short story fragments, n.d.

2 items : 7 p.
Typescript. First fragment titled; fragments
probably from same draft. Missing p. 6–7 and
ending. Signed "Alice Laidlaw Munro".

MUNRO, ALICE, 1931–   Msc 37.6.62
Dance of the happy shades : Thanks for the
ride : short story fragment, n.d.

1 item : 6 p.
Typescript ending fragment.

MUNRO, ALICE, 1931–   Msc 37.6.63
Thanks for the ride.
p. 1, 25–37.

Detached from Tamarack Review, no. 2, Winter 1957.
Includes holograph annotation "1957" on title page.

MUNRO, ALICE, 1931–   Msc 37.6.64
The time of death.
p. 49, 63–66.

Detached from Canadian Forum, v. 36, no. 425, June
1956. Includes holograph annotation "1956" on the
title page. Author shown as Alice Laidlaw, maiden
name of A. Munro.

MUNRO, ALICE, 1931–   MsC 37.7.1
Dance of the happy shades : A trip to the
coast : short story fragment, n.d.

1 item : 5 p.
Typescript beginning fragment titled The trip to the
coast, later published as A trip to the coast.

MUNRO, ALICE, 1931–   MsC 37.7.2
Dance of the happy shades : A trip to the
coast : short story fragments, n.d.

6 items : 30 p. on 29 leaves.
Typescript.   Untitled fragments from various
versions.

MUNRO, ALICE, 1931–   MsC 37.7.3
Dance of the happy shades : A trip to the
coast : short story fragment, n.d.

1 item : 15 p.
Typescript with holograph revisions.   Beginning
fragment titled Trip to the coast, later published as
A trip to the coast.

MUNRO, ALICE, 1931–   MsC 37.7.4
Dance of the happy shades : A trip to the
coast : short story fragment, n.d.

1 item : 1 p.
Typescript fragment, possibly originally part of
MsC 37.7.5.

MUNRO, ALICE, 1931–   MsC 37.7.5
Dance of the happy shades: A trip to the
coast : short story, n.d.

1 item : 25 p.
Typescript.   Titled The trip to the coast, also
published as A trip to the coast.   Signed "Alice
Munro".

MUNRO, ALICE, 1931–   MsC 37.7.6
   Dance of the happy shades : A trip to the
   coast : short story, n.d.

   1 item : 15 p.
   Typescript (carbon copy) with holograph revisions.
   Titled The trip to the coast, also published as A
   trip to the coast. Holograph address and telephone
   numbers on verso of last page.

MUNRO, ALICE, 1931–   MsC 37.7.7
   Dance of the happy shades : A trip to the
   coast : short story fragment, n.d.

   1 item : 7 p.
   Typescript. Beginning fragment titled The trip to
   the coast, also published as A trip to the coast.

MUNRO, ALICE, 1931–   MsC 37.7.8
   Dance of the happy shades : A trip to the
   coast : short story fragments, n.d.

   3 items : 3 p.
   Typescript fragments. Untitled.

MUNRO, ALICE, 1931–   MsC 37.7.9
   Dance of the happy shades : A trip to the
   coast : short story, n.d.

   1 item : 17 p.
   Typescript with holograph deletions. Titled The trip
   to the coast, also published as A trip to the coast.
   Signed "Alice Munro". Page 5 damaged, missing
   part of text.

MUNRO, ALICE, 1931–   MsC 37.7.10
    Dance of the happy shades : Walker Brothers
    cowboy : short story fragments, n.d.

    5 items : 7 p.
    Typescript and typescript with holograph revision.
    Untitled fragments possibly related to early versions
    of Walker Brothers cowboy.

MUNRO, ALICE, 1931–   MsC 37.7.11
    Dance of the happy shades : Walker Brothers
    cowboy : short story fragment, n.d.

    1 item : 9 p. on 8 leaves.
    Typescript with holograph revisions.   Untitled.

MUNRO, ALICE, 1931–   MsC 37.7.12
    Dance of the happy shades : Walker Brothers
    cowboy : short story fragment, n.d.

    1 item : 16 p.
    Typescript.   Untitled beginning fragment.

MUNRO, ALICE, 1931–   MsC 37.7.13
    Dance of the happy shades : Walker Brothers
    cowboy : short story fragments, n.d.

    5 items : 13 p.
    Typescript and typescript with holograph revisions.
    Untitled fragments from various drafts.

MUNRO, ALICE, 1931–   MsC 37.7.14
    Dance of the happy shades : Walker Brothers
    cowboy : short story fragments, n.d.

    2 items : 3 p.
    Typescript and typescript with holograph revisions.
    Untitled fragments.

MUNRO, ALICE, 1931-   MsC 37.7.15
Dance of the happy shades : Walker Brothers
cowboy : short story, 1967.

1 item : 16 p.
Typescript (photocopy). Copy edited. Signed
"Alice Munro". Includes repository photocopy of
covering letter (original MsC 37.2.39.2) from Earle
Toppings, Ryerson Press, indicating that Walker
Brothers cowboy will be published in "the book",
probably Dance of the happy shades.

MUNRO, ALICE, 1931-   MsC 37.7.16
Walker Brothers cowboy.
p. 106-108, 110-111.

Detached from Harper's Queen, July 1976.

MUNRO, ALICE, 1931-   MsC 37.7.17
Dance of the happy shades : contents list, n.d.

1 item : 1 p.
Holograph. List of short story titles, probably
those considered for inclusion in Dance of the happy
shades.

MUNRO, ALICE, 1931-   MsC 37.7.18
Dance of the happy shades : Canadian reviews,
n.d., 1968 October 19-1970 Spring.

29 items : 61 p.
Newsclippings and photocopies of reviews from
newspapers and periodicals published in Canada.
Also includes two radio reviews, one of which
contains Earle Toppings's holograph annotation
"Alice - You may have heard this on Anthology.
A lovely review. All happy wishes, Earle -
Nov. 27/68". Radio reviews precede those from
newspapers and journals, which are arranged
chronologically. Includes duplicates of many
reviews.

MUNRO, ALICE, 1931–   MsC 37.7.19
    Dance of the happy shades : American reviews,
    n.d., 1973 August 12–1974 June 9.

    29 items : 33 p.
    Newsclippings and photocopies of reviews from
    newspapers and periodicals published in the United
    States. Includes some duplicates. Items arranged
    chronologically.

MUNRO, ALICE, 1931–   MsC 37.7.20
    Dance of the happy shades : British reviews, n.d.,
    1974 May 2–1974 June 13.

    7 items : 7 p.
    Photocopies of reviews from newspapers and
    periodicals published in Great Britain. Arranged
    chronologically.

WEAVER, ROBERT.   MsC 37.7.21
    Canadian short stories : reviews, n.d.,
    1960 June 25–1961 Spring.

    30 items : 36 p.
    Photocopies of reviews of the anthology Canadian
    short stories. (Selected by Robert Weaver.
    London: Oxford University Press, 1960.) From
    various newspapers and periodicals; also includes
    two radio reviews. Alice Munro's short story The
    time of death published in the anthology. Items
    arranged chronologically.

WEAVER, ROBERT.   MsC 37.7.22
    The first five years : a selection from the
    Tamarack Review : reviews, n.d.,
    1962 November 10–1963 January 19.

    16 items : 13 p.
    Photocopies of reviews of The first five years : a
    selection from the Tamarack Review. (Edited by
    Robert Weaver. Toronto: Oxford University Press,
    1962.) From various newspapers as well as one
    radio review. Anthology includes Alice Munro's The
    Peace of Utrecht. Items arranged chronologically.

WEAVER, ROBERT.   MsC 37.7.23
    Canadian short stories : second series : reviews,
    1968 November 30.

    1 item : 1 p.
    Newsclipping and photocopy of review of Canadian
    short stories : second series. (Selected by Robert
    Weaver. Toronto: Oxford University Press, 1968.)
    Anthology includes Alice Munro's short stories Dance
    of the happy shades and The Peace of Utrecht.

MUNRO, ALICE, 1931-   MsC 37.7.24
    Something I've been meaning to tell
    you : Executioners : short story fragments, n.d.

    2 items : 4 p.
    Typescript. Untitled fragments with segments
    possibly related to Executioners.

MUNRO, ALICE, 1931-   MsC 37.7.25
    Something I've been meaning to tell you : Places at
    home : short story fragment, n.d.

    1 item : 13 p.
    Typescript with holograph revisions. Titled
    fragment. Published as Executioners.

MUNRO, ALICE, 1931-   MsC 37.7.26
    Something I've been meaning to tell you : The heart
    of an executioner : short story fragment, n.d.

    1 item : 23 p.
    Typescript with holograph revisions. Titled
    fragment. Published as Executioners.

MUNRO, ALICE, 1931-   MsC 37.7.27
    Something I've been meaning to tell
    you : Executioners : short story fragment, n.d.

    1 item : 19 p.
    Typescript. Titled fragment, missing ending.

MUNRO, ALICE, 1931–   MsC 37.7.28
    Something I've been meaning to tell
    you : Executioners, short story fragment, n.d.

    1 item : 14 p.
    Typescript and typescript (photocopy). Pages 4-14
    are photocopies of MsC 37.7.27. Titled fragment,
    with ending missing.

MUNRO, ALICE, 1931–   MsC 37.7.29
    Something I've been meaning to tell
    you : Executioners : short story fragment, n.d.

    1 item : 1 p.
    Typescript. Ending fragment, possibly from
    MsC 37.7.28.

MUNRO, ALICE, 1931–   MsC 37.7.30
    Something I've been meaning to tell
    you : Executioners : short story fragments, n.d.

    2 items : 9 p.
    Typescript with holograph corrections. Pages 8-15,
    21; probably originally part of MsC 37.7.32.

MUNRO, ALICE, 1931–   MsC 37.7.31
    Something I've been meaning to tell
    you : Executioners : short story, n.d.

    1 item : 21 p.
    Typescript (photocopy). Titled. Pages 1-7
    photocopies of MsC 37.7.32 before copy editing;
    p. 8-15, 21 photocopies of MsC 37.7.30.

MUNRO, ALICE, 1931–   MsC 37.7.32
    Something I've been meaning to tell
    you : Executioners : short story fragments, n.d.

    2 items : 18 p.
    Typescript with holograph revisions. Copy edited.
    Untitled fragments, probably from same draft;
    missing p. 16-19.

MUNRO, ALICE, 1931–   MsC 37.7.33
    Something I've been meaning to tell
    you : Executioners : short story fragments, n.d.

    2 items : 9 p.
    Typescript (photocopy). Two fragments photocopied
    from draft of Executioners found in MsC 37.9.2, the
    manuscript for short story collection Something I've
    been meaning to tell you. Copied prior to copy
    editing.

MUNRO, ALICE, 1931–   MsC 37.7.34
    Something I've been meaning to tell
    you : Forgiveness in families : short story, n.d.

    1 item : 10 p.
    Typescript with holograph addition. Untitled.

MUNRO, ALICE, 1931–   MsC 37.7.35
    Forgiveness in families : short story, n.d.

    1 item : 10 p.
    Typescript (photocopy). Forwarded by Canadian
    Broadcasting Corporation. Covering letter from
    Robert Weaver indicates that Forgiveness in families
    had been broadcast, probably on radio program
    Anthology, March 10, 1973. Includes repository
    photocopy of covering letter (original
    MsC 37.2.8.10).

MUNRO, ALICE, 1931–   MsC 37.7.36
    Something I've been meaning to tell
    you : Forgiveness in families : short story, n.d.

    1 item : 14 p.
    Typescript with holograph correction. Titled.

MUNRO, ALICE, 1931–   MsC 37.7.37
    Forgiveness in families.
    p. 92–93, 138, 140, 142, 144, 146.

    In McCall's, v. 101, no. 7, April 1974.

MUNRO, ALICE, 1931–   MsC 37.7.38
Something I've been meaning to tell you : The found
boat : short story fragments, n.d.

4 items : 15 p.
Typescript and typescript with holograph revisions.
Untitled fragments with sections possibly related to
early versions of The found boat.

MUNRO, ALICE, 1931–   MsC 37.7.39
Something I've been meaning to tell you : The found
boat : short story, n.d.

1 item : 12 p.
Typescript with holograph revisions.   Untitled.

MUNRO, ALICE, 1931–   MsC 37.7.40
Something I've been going to tell you : The found
boat : short story, n.d.

1 item : 13 p.
Typescript.   Titled.   Signed "Alice Munro".

MUNRO, ALICE, 1931–   MsC 37.7.41
Something I've been going to tell you : The found
boat : short story, n.d.

1 item : 13 p.
Typescript.   Titled.

MUNRO, ALICE, 1931–   MsC 37.8.1
Something I've been meaning to tell you : How I met
my husband : first draft, n.d.

1 item : 24 p.
Typescript.   Titled.   Holograph annotation "First
Draft" on verso of last page.

MUNRO, ALICE, 1931–   MsC 37.8.2
    Something I've been meaning to tell you : How I met
    my husband : short story, n.d.

    1 item : 23 p.
    Typescript with some errors marked. Titled.
    Includes holograph annotation "Edie" on title page.

MUNRO, ALICE, 1931–   MsC 37.8.3
    Something I've been meaning to tell
    you : Marrakesh : short story fragment, n.d.

    1 item : 9 p.
    Typescript with holograph revisions. Untitled
    beginning fragment.

MUNRO, ALICE, 1931–   MsC 37.8.4
    Something I've been meaning to tell
    you : Marrakesh : short story fragment, n.d.

    1 item : 7 p.
    Typescript. Ending fragment.

MUNRO, ALICE, 1931–   MsC 37.8.5
    Something I've been meaning to tell
    you : Ambassador from Marrakesh : short story,
    n.d.

    1 item : 15 p.
    Typescript. Titled Ambassador from Marrakesh,
    published as Marrakesh. Signed "Alice Munro".

MUNRO, ALICE, 1931–   MsC 37.8.6
    Something I've been meaning to tell
    you : Ambassador from Marrakesh : short story
    fragment, n.d.

    1 item : 18 p.
    Typescript. Last page missing. Titled Ambassador
    from Marrakesh, published as Marrakesh.

MUNRO, ALICE, 1931–   MsC 37.8.7
    Something I've been meaning to tell
you : Marrakesh : short story fragment, n.d.

    1 item : 2 p.
Typescript (photocopy). Variant ending, probably
for MsC 37.8.6.

MUNRO, ALICE, 1931–   MsC 37.8.8
    Something I've been meaning to tell you : Real
people : short story, 196-.

    1 item : 14 p.
Typescript. Identified by A. Munro, February 14,
1981, as an early version of Material, written in the
1960s.

MUNRO, ALICE, 1931–   MsC 37.8.9
    Something I've been meaning to tell
you : Material : short story fragment, n.d.

    1 item : 6 p.
Typescript. Untitled beginning fragment.

MUNRO, ALICE, 1931–   MsC 37.8.10
    Something I've been meaning to tell
you : Material : short story, n.d.

    1 item : 20 p.
Typescript with holograph revisions. Holograph
title.

MUNRO, ALICE, 1931–   MsC 37.8.11
    Something I've been meaning to tell
you : Material : short story fragment, n.d.

    1 item : 3 p.
Typescript with holograph revision. Variant ending
fragment.

MUNRO, ALICE, 1931–   MsC 37.8.12
Something I've been meaning to tell
you : Material : short story, n.d.

1 item : 22 p.
Typescript with holograph corrections. Titled.

MUNRO, ALICE, 1931–   MsC 37.8.13
Something I've been meaning to tell
you : Memorial : short story fragment, n.d.

1 item : 9 p.
Typescript with holograph revisions. Untitled early
version.

MUNRO, ALICE, 1931–   MsC 37.8.14
Something I've been meaning to tell
you : Memorial : short story fragment, n.d.

1 item : 5 p.
Typescript with holograph revisions. Untitled
beginning fragment.

MUNRO, ALICE, 1931–   MsC 37.8.15
Something I've been meaning to tell
you : Memorial : short story fragments, n.d.

2 items : 4 p.
Typescript. Untitled beginning fragments.

MUNRO, ALICE, 1931–   MsC 37.8.16
Something I've been meaning to tell
you : Memorial : short story, n.d.

1 item : 19 p.
Typescript with holograph revisions. Titled.

MUNRO, ALICE, 1931–   MsC 37.8.17
     Something I've been meaning to tell
     you : Memorial : short story, n.d.

     1 item : 21 p.
     Typescript. Typing and spelling errors marked.
     Titled.

MUNRO, ALICE, 1931–   MsC 37.8.18
     Something I've been meaning to tell
     you : Memorial : short story fragments, n.d.

     2 items : 2 p.
     Typescript with holograph revisions. Pages 17,
     21; possibly revised pages for MsC 37.8.17.

MUNRO, ALICE, 1931–   MsC 37.8.19
     Something I've been meaning to tell
     you : Memorial : short story fragments, n.d.

     2 items : 6 p.
     Typescript with copy editing and typescript
     (photocopy). Titled beginning fragments; the
     second is a copy of the first before copy editing.

MUNRO, ALICE, 1931–   MsC 37.8.20
     Something I've been meaning to tell you : The
     Ottawa Valley : short story, n.d.

     1 item : 18 p.
     Typescript with holograph revisions. Titled.

MUNRO, ALICE, 1931–   MsC 37.8.21
     Something I've been meaning to tell you : Something
     I've been meaning to tell you : short story
     fragment, n.d.

     1 item : 11 p.
     Typescript with holograph revisions. Untitled
     fragment, possibly related to early versions of
     Something I've been meaning to tell you.

MUNRO, ALICE, 1931–   MSC 37.8.22
    Something I've been meaning to tell you : Something
    I've been meaning to tell you : short story
    fragments, n.d.

    2 items : 14 p.
    Typescript with holograph revisions.   Untitled
    fragments, possibly from same draft.

MUNRO, ALICE, 1931–   MsC 37.8.23
    Something I've been meaning to tell you : Et and
    Char : short story, n.d.

    1 item : 26 p.
    Typescript with holograph revisions.   Titled Et and
    Char, published as Something I've been meaning to
    tell you.

MUNRO, ALICE, 1931–   MsC 37.8.24
    Something I've been meaning to tell you : Something
    I've been meaning to tell you : short story, n.d.

    1 item : 23 p.
    Typescript with holograph deletion.   Titled.

MUNRO, ALICE, 1931–   MsC 37.8.25
    Something I've been meaning to tell you : The
    Spanish lady : short story fragments, n.d.

    4 items : 21 p.
    Typescript and typescript with holograph revisions.
    Untitled fragments with sections possibly related to
    early versions of The Spanish lady.

MUNRO, ALICE, 1931–   MsC 37.8.26
    Something I've been meaning to tell you : The
    Spanish lady : short story fragment, n.d.

    1 item : 3 p.
    Typescript with holograph revisions.   Untitled
    fragment, possibly part of an early version of
    The Spanish lady.

MUNRO, ALICE, 1931–   MsC 37.8.27
Something I've been meaning to tell you : The
Spanish lady : short story, n.d.

1 item : 15 p.
Typescript with holograph revisions. Untitled.

MUNRO, ALICE, 1931–   MsC 37.8.28
Something I've been meaning to tell you : The
Spaniard's lady : short story, n.d.

1 item : 15 p.
Typescript with holograph revisions. Titled The
Spaniard's lady, published as The Spanish lady.
Signed "Alice Munro".

MUNRO, ALICE, 1931–   MsC 37.8.29
Something I've been meaning to tell you : The
Spanish lady : short story, n.d.

1 item : 19 p.
Typescript with holograph revisions. Titled.

MUNRO, ALICE, 1931–   MsC 37.8.30
Something I've been meaning to tell you : Tell me
yes or no : short story fragment, n.d.

1 item : 2 p.
Typescript. Untitled fragment, possibly related to
early versions of Tell me yes or no.

MUNRO, ALICE, 1931–   MsC 37.8.31
Something I've been meaning to tell you : Tell me
yes or no : short story fragment, n.d.

1 item : 8 p.
Typescript. Untitled fragment, possibly related to
early versions of Tell me yes or no.

MUNRO, ALICE, 1931–   MsC 37.8.32
Something I've been meaning to tell you : Tell me
yes or no : short story, n.d.

1 item : 18 p.
Typescript with holograph revisions. Titled. Page
15 apparently inserted after completion of draft.

MUNRO, ALICE, 1931–   MsC 37.8.33
Something I've been meaning to tell you : Tell me
yes or no : short story fragment, n.d.

1 item : 1 p.
Typescript. Titled beginning fragment.

MUNRO, ALICE, 1931–   MsC 37.8.34
Something I've been meaning to tell you : Tell me
yes or no : short story fragments, n.d.

2 items : 2 p.
Typescript. Variant ending fragments.

MUNRO, ALICE, 1931–   MsC 37.8.35
Something I've been meaning to tell you : Tell me
yes or no : short story, n.d.

1 item : 19 p.
Typescript. Titled. Spelling and typing errors
marked.

MUNRO, ALICE, 1931–   MsC 37.8.36
Something I've been meaning to tell you : Tell me
yes or no : short story fragment, n.d.

1 item : 13 p.
Typescript (photocopy). Ending fragment.
Photocopy of p. 122–134 in collected short story
manuscript of Something I've been meaning to tell
you (MsC 37.9.1) before copy editing.

MUNRO, ALICE, 1931–   MsC 37.8.37
    Something I've been meaning to tell you : Walking on
    water : short story fragments, n.d.

    6 items : 23 p.
    Typescript and typescript with holograph revisions.
    Untitled fragments possibly related to early versions
    of Walking on water.

MUNRO, ALICE, 1931–   MsC 37.8.38
    Something I've been meaning to tell you : Walking on
    water : short story, n.d.

    1 item : 25 p.
    Typescript. Untitled.

MUNRO, ALICE, 1931–   MsC 37.8.39
    Something I've been meaning to tell you : Walking on
    water : short story, n.d.

    1 item : 24 p.
    Typescript with holograph revisions. Edited for
    spelling errors. Titled.

MUNRO, ALICE, 1931–   MsC 37.8.40
    Something I've been meaning to tell you : Walking on
    water : short story fragments, n.d.

    2 items : 17 p.
    Typescript (photocopy). Titled. Photocopy of
    p. 77–91, 97, 98 in collected short story manuscript
    of Something I've been meaning to tell you
    (MsC 37.9.1) before copy editing. Includes
    holograph annotation "4th & final" on first page of
    second fragment.

MUNRO, ALICE, 1931-   MsC 37.8.41
    Ten stories by Alice Munro : Mr   : short story,
    1973.

    1 item : 26 p.
    Typescript (photocopy) with h.. ..ᵤᵣ ᵖh corrections.
    Titled. Photocopy of p. 24-49 in collected short
    story manuscript of Something I've been meaning to
    tell you (MsC 37.9.1) before copy editing and
    revisions. Manuscript is one of three originally filed
    in a McGraw-Hill Ryerson Limited folder with the
    annotation "Ten Stories by Alice Munro (all stories
    (c) Copyright: Alice Munro 1973)". Holograph
    annotations "(c) Copyright: Alice Munro, 1973" and
    "Return to McGraw-Hill Ryerson Limited" on title
    page. Manuscripts from folder are filed in order
    found.

MUNRO, ALICE, 1931-   MsC 37.8.42
    Ten stories by Alice Munro : How I met my
    husband : short story, 1973.

    1 item : 23 p.
    Typescript with holograph revisions (photocopy).
    Titled. Photocopy of MsC 37.8.2. Manuscript is one
    of three originally filed in a McGraw-Hill Ryerson
    Limited folder with the annotation "Ten Stories by
    Alice Munro (all stories (c) Copyright: Alice Munro
    1973)". Holograph annotations "(c) Copyright:
    Alice Munro, 1973" and "Return to McGraw-Hill
    Ryerson Limited" on title page. Manuscripts from
    folder are filed in order found.

MUNRO, ALICE, 1931-   MsC 37.8.43
    Ten stories by Alice Munro : Forgiveness in
    families : short story, 1973.

    1 item : 16 p.
    Typescript (photocopy) with holograph corrections.
    Titled. Photocopy of p. 100-115 in collected short
    story manuscript of Something I've been meaning to
    tell you (MsC 37.9.1) before copy editing and
    revisions. Manuscript is one of three originally filed
    in a McGraw-Hill Ryerson Limited folder with the
    annotation "Ten Stories by Alice Munro (all stories
    (c) Copyright: Alice Munro 1973)". Holograph
    annotations "(c) Copyright: Alice Munro, 1973" and
    "Return to: McGraw-Hill Ryerson Limited" on title
    page. Manuscripts from folder are filed in order
    found.

MUNRO, ALICE, 1931–   Msc 37.8.44
   Ten stories by Alice Munro : The found boat : short
   story fragment, 1973.

   1 item : 14 p.
   Typescript (photocopy) with holograph corrections.
   Titled. Photocopy of p. 135–148 in collected short
   story manuscript of Something I've been meaning to
   tell you (MsC 37.9.2) before copy editing and
   revisions. Last page missing. Manuscript probably
   part of Ten stories by Alice Munro; tentatively
   identified by holograph annotations "(c) Copyright:
   Alice Munro, 1973" and "Return to McGraw-Hill
   Ryerson Limited" on title page. Filed alphabetically
   by title with other short stories from this group
   found loose in the collection.

MUNRO, ALICE, 1931–   Msc 37.8.45
   Ten stories by Alice Munro : Marrakesh : short
   story fragment, 1973(?).

   1 item : 2 p.
   Typescript (photocopy) with holograph revisions.
   Photocopy of p. 15–16 of draft in MsC 37.8.6.
   Fragment probably originally part of Marrakesh draft
   in collected short story manuscript of Something I've
   been meaning to tell you (p. 179–180 in MsC 37.9.2).
   (Marrakesh draft found in the collected short story
   manuscript probably at one time part of Ten stories
   by Alice Munro.) Fragment filed alphabetically by
   title along with other short stories from this group
   found loose in the collection.

MUNRO, ALICE, 1931–   Msc 37.8.46
   Ten stories by Alice Munro : Memorial : short story
   fragment, 1973(?).

   1 item : 18 p.
   Typescript (photocopy) with holograph revisions.
   Copy edited for publisher. Photocopy of p. 4–21 of
   draft in MsC 37.8.17. Manuscript probably part of
   Ten stories by Alice Munro. Filed alphabetically by
   title with other short stories from this group found
   loose in the collection.

MUNRO, ALICE, 1931–   MsC 37.8.47
Ten stories by Alice Munro : Tell me yes or
no : short story fragments, 1973(?).

2 items : 11 p.
Typescript (photocopy) with holograph revisions.
Photocopy of p. 7-10, 12-18 of draft in MsC 37.8.35.
Fragment probably originally part of Tell me yes or
no in the collected short story manuscript of
Something I've been meaning to tell you (p. 122-125,
127-133 in MsC 37.9.1). (Draft of Tell me yes or no
in that collected short story manuscript probably at
one time included in Ten stories by Alice Munro.)
Fragment filed alphabetically by title with others
from this group found loose in the collection.

MUNRO, ALICE, 1931–   MsC 37.8.48
Ten stories by Alice Munro : Walking on
water : short story, 1973.

1 item : 24 p.
Typescript (photocopy) with holograph revisions.
Photocopy of MsC 37.8.39. Manuscript probably part
of Ten stories by Alice Munro; tentatively identified
by holograph annotations "(c) Copyright: Alice
Munro, 1973" and "Return to McGraw-Hill Ryerson
Limited" on title page. Holograph annotation "3rd"
on p. 22. Filed alphabetically by title with other
short stories from this group found loose in the
papers.

MUNRO, ALICE, 1931–   MsC 37.9.1-2
Something I've been meaning to tell you : short
stories, 1973(?).

1 item : 135 p; 117 p.
Typescript and typescript (photocopy) with
holograph revisions. Copy edited for publisher.
Holograph galley numbers at tops of some pages.
Holograph title page reads "Munro/Stories". Several
of the short story manuscripts were probably at one
time part of Ten stories by Alice Munro, identified
by holograph annotations "(c) Copyright: Alice
Munro, 1973" and "Return to McGraw-Hill Ryerson
Limited" on title pages. Position of Winter wind in
the manuscript is different from published version.

MUNRO, ALICE, 1931–   MsC 37.9.3
    Something I've been meaning to tell you : Canadian
    reviews, n.d., 1974 January 6–1975 June.

    27 items : 34 p.
    Newsclippings and photocopies of reviews from
    various Canadian newspapers and periodicals, as well
    as one radio review. Also includes a photocopy of
    an article by Robert Fulford discussing Tamarack
    Review, no. 61, and A. Munro's short story
    Material, which was published in that issue of the
    journal. Arranged chronologically.

MUNRO, ALICE, 1931–   MsC 37.9.4
    Something I've been meaning to tell you : American
    reviews, 1974 September 22–1975 March 30.

    16 items : 22 p. on 21 leaves.
    Newsclipping and photocopies of reviews from various
    newspapers and a periodical published in the United
    States. Arranged chronologically.

MUNRO, ALICE, 1931–   MsC 37.9.5
    Who do you think you are? : The beggar
    maid : short story fragments, n.d.

    2 items : 19 p.
    Typescript and typescript with holograph revisions.
    Untitled fragments from early versions.

MUNRO, ALICE, 1931–   MsC 37.9.6
    Who do you think you are? : The beggar
    maid : short story fragment, n.d.

    1 item : 4 p.
    Typescript with holograph revisions. Untitled
    fragment from early version.

MUNRO, ALICE, 1931–   MsC 37.9.7
   Who do you think you are? : The beggar
   maid : short story fragments, n.d.

   4 items : 10 p.
   Holograph and typescript. Untitled fragments from
   early versions. Pages in item 1 may not be
   consecutive; fragments 3 and 4 probably
   consecutive. Holograph annotation on verso of first
   page of fragment 3. 3 p. holograph, 7 p.
   typescript.

MUNRO, ALICE, 1931–   MsC 37.9.8
   Who do you think you are? : The beggar
   maid : short story fragments, n.d.

   4 items : 5 p.
   Typescript. Untitled fragments with sections related
   to The beggar maid.

MUNRO, ALICE, 1931–   MsC 37.9.9
   Who do you think you are? : The beggar
   maid : short story fragments, n.d.

   7 items : 18 p.
   Typescript and typescript with holograph revisions.
   Untitled fragments with sections possibly related to
   The beggar maid.

MUNRO, ALICE, 1931–   MsC 37.9.10
   Who do you think you are? : The beggar
   maid : short story fragment, n.d.

   1 item : 2 p.
   Holograph. Untitled fragment, possibly related to
   The beggar maid.

MUNRO, ALICE, 1931–   MsC 37.9.11
  Who do you think you are? : The beggar
  maid : short story fragments, n.d.

  5 items : 12 p.
  Typescript and typescript with holograph revisions.
  Untitled fragments from early versions.

MUNRO, ALICE, 1931–   MsC 37.9.12
  Who do you think you are? : The beggar
  maid : short story fragments, n.d.

  4 items : 8 p. on 7 leaves.
  Typescript. Untitled fragments. Holograph story
  outline on verso of last page of item 3.

MUNRO, ALICE, 1931–   MsC 37.9.13
  Who do you think you are? : The beggar
  maid : short story fragments, n.d.

  2 items : 17 p.
  Typescript. Untitled fragments.

MUNRO, ALICE, 1931–   MsC 37.9.14
  Who do you think you are? : The beggar
  maid : short story, n.d.

  1 item : 30 p. on 28 leaves.
  Typescript with holograph additions and revisions.
  Holograph title.

MUNRO, ALICE, 1931–   MsC 37.9.15
  Who do you think you are? : The beggar
  maid : short story fragments, n.d.

  3 items : 3 p.
  Typescript. Variant ending fragments, probably for
  MsC 37.9.14.

MUNRO, ALICE, 1931–   MsC 37.9.16
Who do you think you are? : The beggar
maid : short story, n.d.

1 item : 29 p.
Typescript with holograph corrections. Titled.
Includes photocopy of the item. 29 p. typescript
(photocopy).

MUNRO, ALICE, 1931–   MsC 37.9.17
Who do you think you are? : The beggar
maid : short story fragment, n.d.

1 item : 1 p.
Typescript. Variant ending fragment, probably for
MsC 37.9.16.

MUNRO, ALICE, 1931–   MsC 37.9.18
Notes on Mame Pinning : research notes,
1975 April 19.

1 item : 2 p. on 1 leaf.
Holograph. Author unidentified. Notes on a woman
called Mame Pinning, possibly used by A. Munro as
basis for Flo's background in Half a grapefruit.

MUNRO, ALICE, 1931–   MsC 37.9.19
Who do you think you are? : Half a
grapefruit : short story fragments, n.d.

4 items : 15 p.
Typescript and typescript with holograph revisions.
Untitled fragments with sections related to Half a
grapefruit, Wild swans and Spelling. Fragments 3
and 4 possibly consecutive.

MUNRO, ALICE, 1931–   MsC 37.9.20
Who do you think you are? : Half a
grapefruit : short story fragments, n.d.

2 items : 2 p.
Typescript. Holograph title on first fragment;
second fragment untitled.

MUNRO, ALICE, 1931–   MsC 37.9.21
    Who do you think you are? : Half a
    grapefruit : short story, n.d.

    2 items : 17 p.
    Typescript with holograph revisions. Untitled.
    Includes two variant endings. Incorporates material
    later published as Characters.

MUNRO, ALICE, 1931–   MsC 37.9.22
    Who do you think you are? : Half a
    grapefruit : short story, n.d.

    1 item : 15 p.
    Typescript (photocopy). Titled Half-a-grapefruit.
    Photocopy of MsC 37.9.23 before revisions. Virginia
    Barber sticker on first page. Includes photocopy of
    the item with holograph annotation "1st version" on
    title page. 15 p. typescript (photocopy).

MUNRO, ALICE, 1931–   MsC 37.9.23
    Who do you think you are? : Half a
    grapefruit : short story, n.d.

    1 item : 16 p. on 15 leaves.
    Typescript with holograph revisions. Titled
    Half-a-grapefruit.

MUNRO, ALICE, 1931–   MsC 37.9.24
    Who do you think you are? : Half a
    grapefruit : short story fragment, n.d.

    1 item : 1 p.
    Typescript fragment, possibly originally part (p.9)
    of MsC 37.9.23.

MUNRO, ALICE, 1931–   MsC 37.9.25
    Who do you think you are? : Half a
    grapefruit : short story, n.d.

    1 item : 16 p.
    Typescript. Titled Half-a-grapefruit. Probably a
    clean copy of MsC 37.9.23 after revisions.

MUNRO, ALICE, 1931–   MsC 37.9.26
Who do you think you are? : Half a
grapefruit : short story, n.d.

1 item : 16 p.
Typescript (photocopy) with holograph revisions and
deletions. Titled. Photocopy before revisions of
Half a grapefruit (p. 49–63) in MsC 37.12.29,
manuscript of short story collection Who do you
think you are?. Signed "Alice Munro". Holograph
annotation "Sold to Redbook" on title page.

MUNRO, ALICE, 1931–   MsC 37.9.27
Who do you think you are? : Half a
grapefruit : short story, n.d.

1 item : 23 p.
Typescript with holograph revisions. Titled. Page
21 missing; p. 24 renumbered to p. 22, suggesting
revised ending. Probably a clean copy of p. 40–56
in MsC 37.12.24, manuscript of the short story
collection Who do you think you are?.

MUNRO, ALICE, 1931–   MsC 37.10.1
Who do you think you are? : Mischief : short story
fragment, n.d.

1 item : 2 p.
Typescript. Untitled fragment, possibly related to
early versions of Mischief.

MUNRO, ALICE, 1931–   MsC 37.10.2
Who do you think you are? : Mischief : short story
fragments, n.d.

2 items : 3 p.
Typescript with holograph revisions. Untitled
fragments, possibly related to early versions of
Mischief. Fragments possibly consecutive.

MUNRO, ALICE, 1931–   MsC 37.10.3
    Who do you think you are? : Mischief : short story
    fragment, n.d.

    1 item : 4 p.
    Typescript. Untitled fragment, possibly related to
    early versions of Mischief.

MUNRO, ALICE, 1931–   MsC 37.10.4
    Who do you think you are? : Mischief : short story
    fragment, n.d.

    1 item : 2 p.
    Holograph. Untitled fragment, possibly related to
    early versions of Mischief.

MUNRO, ALICE, 1931–   MsC 37.10.5
    Who do you think you are? : Mischief : short story
    fragments, n.d.

    2 items : 5 p.
    Typescript. Untitled fragments, possibly related to
    early versions of Mischief.

MUNRO, ALICE, 1931–   MsC 37.10.6
    Who do you think you are? : Mischief : short story
    fragment, n.d.

    1 item : 1 p.
    Typescript. Untitled fragment, possibly related to
    early versions of Mischief.

MUNRO, ALICE, 1931–   MsC 37.10.7
    Who do you think you are? : Mischief : short story
    fragment, n.d.

    1 item : 8 p.
    Typescript with holograph revisions. Untitled
    fragment related to early versions of Mischief.

MUNRO, ALICE, 1931–   MsC 37.10.8
Who do you think you are? : Mischief : short story
fragment, n.d.

1 item : 10 p.
Typescript. Titled.

MUNRO, ALICE, 1931–   MsC 37.10.9
Who do you think you are? : Mischief : short story,
n.d.

4 items : 27 p.
Typescript with holograph revisions. Holograph
title. Fragments possibly consecutive, producing
complete draft.

MUNRO, ALICE, 1931–   MsC 37.10.10
Who do you think you are? : Mischief : short story,
n.d.

1 item : 28 p.
Typescript with holograph corrections. Titled.
Signed "Alice Munro". Unidentified holograph
comments on several pages. Holograph annotations
on verso of p. 20.

MUNRO, ALICE, 1931–   MsC 37.10.11
Who do you think you are? : Mischief : short story
fragments, n.d.

2 items : 4 p.
Typescript with holograph revisions. Probably
originally part of MsC 37.10.10.

MUNRO, ALICE, 1931–   MsC 37.10.12
Who do you think you are? : Mischief : short story,
n.d.

1 item : 28 p.
Typescript (photocopy). Photocopy of MsC 37.10.10
before revisions and while fragments in MsC 37.10.11
were part of the draft. Bottom line missing on
p. 2.

MUNRO, ALICE, 1931–   MsC 37.10.13
    Who do you think you are? : Mischief : short story
    fragments, n.d.

    3 items : 3 p.
    Typescript (photocopy) and typescript (photocopy)
    with holograph additions. Pages 13, 36, 52 from
    unidentified draft(s).

MUNRO, ALICE, 1931–   MsC 37.10.14-15
    Who do you think you are? : Mischief : short story,
    n.d.

    1 item : 32 p.
    Typescript and typescript (photocopy) with
    holograph revisions; p. 27-32 cut and paste.
    Holograph title. MsC 37.10.15 is a photocopy of
    MsC 37.10.14. 32 p. typescript (photocopy).

MUNRO, ALICE, 1931–   MsC 37.10.16
    Who do you think you are? : Privilege : short story
    fragment, n.d.

    1 item : 2 p.
    Typescript. Untitled fragment, possibly related to
    early versions of Privilege.

MUNRO, ALICE, 1931–   MsC 37.10.17
    Who do you think you are? : Privilege : short story
    fragments, n.d.

    2 items : 2 p.
    Typescript. Untitled fragments, possibly related to
    early versions of Privilege.

MUNRO, ALICE, 1931–   MsC 37.10.18
    Who do you think you are? : Funerals : short story
    fragment, n.d.

    1 item : 2 p.
    Holograph. Titled Funerals. Fragment related to
    early versions of Privilege.

MUNRO, ALICE, 1931–   MsC 37.10.19
Who do you think you are? : Funerals : short story
fragments, n.d.

5 items : 11 p.
Typescript and typescript with holograph revisions.
Two fragments titled Funerals; three fragments
untitled. Material related to early versions of
Privilege.

MUNRO, ALICE, 1931–   MsC 37.10.20
Who do you think you are? : Privilege : short story
fragments, n.d.

2 items : 16 p.
Typescript with holograph revisions. Untitled.
Fragment 2 possibly originally part of fragment 1.

MUNRO, ALICE, 1931–   MsC 37.10.21
Who do you think you are? : Privilege : short story
fragments, n.d.

4 items : 28 p.
Typescript with holograph revisions. Untitled
fragments with sections related to Privilege and
Royal beatings.

MUNRO, ALICE, 1931–   MsC 37.10.22
Who do you think you are? : Privilege : short story
fragment, n.d.

1 item : 7 p.
Typescript. Untitled fragment with sections related
to Privilege and Royal beatings.

MUNRO, ALICE, 1931–   MsC 37.10.23
Who do you think you are? : Privilege : short story,
n.d.

1 item : 14 p.
Typescript. Untitled. Ending similar to material
published in Characters.

MUNRO, ALICE, 1931–   MsC 37.10.24
Who do you think you are? : Privilege : short story
fragments, n.d.

2 items : 5 p.
Typescript. Variant endings which include material
later published in Characters.

MUNRO, ALICE, 1931–   MsC 37.10.25
Who do you think you are? : Privilege : short story
fragments, n.d.

1 item : 2 p.
Typescript. Untitled.

MUNRO, ALICE, 1931–   MsC 37.10.26
Who do you think you are? : Privilege : short story,
n.d.

1 item : 15 p.
Typescript with pencilled underlining. Titled.
Ending includes material later published in
Characters.

MUNRO, ALICE, 1931–   MsC 37.10.27
Who do you think you are? : Privilege : short story,
n.d.

1 item : 16 p. on 15 leaves.
Typescript (photocopy). Photocopy of MsC 37.10.26
before revisions. Titled. Ending includes material
later published in Characters. Verso of last page
has holograph list of stories(?) and unidentified
holograph text.

MUNRO, ALICE, 1931–   MsC 37.10.28
Who do you think you are? : Privilege : short story,
n.d.

1 item : 19 p.
Typescript (photocopy). Titled. Signed "Alice
Munro". Original typescript for p. 18–19 in
following file. Ending includes material later
published in Characters.

MUNRO, ALICE, 1931–   MsC 37.10.29
Who do you think you are? : Privilege : short story
fragments, n.d.

3 items : 6 p.
Typescript and typescript (photocopy). Variant
endings, probably for MsC 37.10.28. Item 1 is the
original from which the ending of MsC 37.10.28 was
copied, and includes material later published in
Characters. Item 3 consists of three copies of one
variant ending.

MUNRO, ALICE, 1931–   MsC 37.10.30
Who do you think you are? : The honeyman's
grand-daughter : short story, n.d.

1 item : 18 p.
Typescript with holograph revisions. Title revised
from The honeyman's daughter to The honeyman's
grand-daughter, later published as Privilege.

MUNRO, ALICE, 1931–   MsC 37.10.31
Who do you think you are? : The honeyman's
daughter : short story, n.d.

1 item : 18 p.
Typescript (photocopy). Photocopy of MsC 37.10.30
before revisions. Titled The honeyman's daughter,
later published as Privilege. Signed "Alice Munro".
Holograph annotation "Virginia Barber" and New
York address on title page.

MUNRO, ALICE, 1931–   MsC 37.10.32
    Who do you think you are? : The honeyman's
    grand-daughter : short story, n.d.

    1 item : 18 p.
    Typescript. Clean copy of MsC 37.10.30 after
    revisions. Titled The honeyman's grand-daughter,
    later published as Privilege.

MUNRO, ALICE, 1931–   MsC 37.10.33
    Who do you think you are? : Privilege : short story
    fragment, n.d.

    1 item : 19 p.
    Typescript with holograph revisions. Revised clean
    copy of the draft of Privilege (p. 24-37) in short
    story collection manuscript of Who do you think you
    are? (MsC 37.12.24). Ending is missing.

MUNRO, ALICE, 1931–   MsC 37.10.34
    Who do you think you are? : Providence : short
    story fragment, n.d.

    1 item : 14 p.
    Typescript. Untitled.

MUNRO, ALICE, 1931–   MsC 37.10.35
    Who do you think you are? : Providence : short
    story, n.d.

    1 item : 14 p.
    Typescript (photocopy). Titled. Signed "Alice
    Munro".

MUNRO, ALICE, 1931–   MsC 37.10.36
    Who do you think you are? : Providence : short
    story, n.d.

    1 item : 13 p.
    Typescript (photocopy) with holograph revisions.
    Titled.

MUNRO, ALICE, 1931–   MsC 37.10.37
   Who do you think you are? : Providence : short
   story fragment, n.d.

   1 item : 2 p.
   Typescript with holograph revisions. Fragment
   probably part of a revised clean copy of the draft of
   Providence (p. 135-152) in short story collection
   manuscript of Who do you think you are?
   (MsC 37.12.24). Holograph number "31" precedes
   page numbers. (For similar pagination see
   MsC 37.10.40 and MsC 37.13.5-6.)

MUNRO, ALICE, 1931–   MsC 37.10.38
   Who do you think you are? : Providence : short
   story fragments, n.d.

   2 items : 5 p.
   Typescript. Titled beginning fragment and ending
   fragment, probably originally part of MsC 37.10.39.

MUNRO, ALICE, 1931–   MsC 37.10.39
   Who do you think you are? : Providence : short
   story, n.d.

   2 items : 18 p.
   Typescript with holograph revisions. Titled.
   Includes one page variant ending. Title page
   includes holograph annotation "Change: Nadine to
   Caroline   Patrick to Dennis".

MUNRO, ALICE, 1931–   MsC 37.10.40
   Who do you think you are? : Providence : short
   story, n.d.

   1 item : 29 p. on 27 leaves.
   Typescript and typescript (photocopy) with
   holograph revisions. Pages 1-11, 18 are revised
   clean copies of pages in MsC 37.10.39; p. 12-17,
   19-27 are revised clean copies (photocopy) of pages
   in the draft of Providence (p. 135-152) in short
   story collection manuscript of Who do you think you
   are? (MsC 37.12.24). Holograph numbers "32" or
   "33" precede some page numbers. (See MsC 37.10.37
   and MsC 37.13.5-6 for similar pagination.)

MUNRO, ALICE, 1931–   MsC 37.10.41
  Who do you think you are? : Royal beatings : short
  story fragments, n.d.

  7 items : 11 p.
  Typescript with holograph additions and revisions.
  Untitled miscellaneous fragments from unidentified
  drafts.

MUNRO, ALICE, 1931–   MsC 37.10.42
  Who do you think you are? : Royal beatings : short
  story fragment, n.d.

  1 item : 15 p.
  Typescript. Untitled. Beginning and ending
  sections are similar to unpublished material titled
  The war hero, the boy murderer, the lady
  ventriloquist.

MUNRO, ALICE, 1931–   MsC 37.10.43
  Who do you think you are? : Royal beatings : short
  story fragment, n.d.

  1 item : 19 p.
  Typescript with holograph revisions. Untitled.
  Includes section similar to that in Spelling.
  Incomplete(?).

MUNRO, ALICE, 1931–   MsC 37.10.44
  Who do you think you are? : Royal beatings : short
  story fragment, n.d.

  1 item : 5 p.
  Typescript with holograph revisions. Untitled.

MUNRO, ALICE, 1931–   MsC 37.10.45
  Who do you think you are? : Royal beatings : short
  story fragments, n.d.

  6 items : 12 p. on 10 leaves.
  Typescript with holograph text on verso of two
  pages. Untitled. Fragments 4, 5, 6 possibly
  continuations of fragment 3.

MUNRO, ALICE, 1931–   MsC 37.11.1
Who do you think you are? : Royal beatings : short
story fragments, n.d.

2 items : 9 p.
Typescript and typescript with holograph addition.
Untitled. Fragments possibly consecutive.

MUNRO, ALICE, 1931–   MsC 37.11.2
Who do you think you are? : Royal beatings : short
story fragment, n.d.

1 item : 20 p. on 19 leaves.
Typescript and holograph. Untitled. Story possibly
complete, with holograph text belonging to a
different draft(?). 1 p. holograph, 19 p.
typescript.

MUNRO, ALICE, 1931–   MsC 37.11.3
Who do you think you are? : Royal beatings : short
story fragments, n.d.

3 items : 5 p.
Typescript; cut and paste revisions in item 3. First
fragment titled. Fragments probably originally part
of MsC 37.11.4.

MUNRO, ALICE, 1931–   MsC 37.11.4
Who do you think you are? : Royal beatings : short
story, n.d.

1 item : 25 p.
Typescript with holograph deletions. Titled.

MUNRO, ALICE, 1931–   MsC 37.11.5
Who do you think you are? : Royal beatings : short
story, n.d.

1 item : 28 p. on 25 leaves.
Typescript (photocopy) with holograph revisions.
Photocopy of MsC 37.11.4. Holograph segments,
numbered 1–6, on verso of p. 24–25. Holograph
annotation "ORIGINAL" on title page.

MUNRO, ALICE, 1931–   MsC 37.11.6
Who do you think you are? : Royal beatings : short
story, n.d.

1 item : 25 p.
Typescript. Titled. Clean copy of MsC 37.11.5.

MUNRO, ALICE, 1931–   MsC 37.11.7
Who do you think you are? : Royal beatings : short
story fragment, n.d.

1 item : 4 p.
Typescript with holograph revisions. Untitled
beginning fragment.

MUNRO, ALICE, 1931–   MsC 37.11.8
Who do you think you are? : Royal beatings : short
story, n.d.

1 item : 30 p.
Typescript and typescript (photocopy). Titled.
Paginated p. 2-31. Revised clean copy of the draft
of Royal beatings (p.2-22) in short story collection
manuscript of Who do you think you are?
(MsC 37.12.24).

MUNRO, ALICE, 1931–   MsC 37.11.9
Royal beatings : galleys, 1977 January 7.

1 item : 19 p.
Copy-edited galleys from the New Yorker. (Royal
beatings published in March 14, 1977 issue of the
New Yorker). Includes repository photocopy of
covering letter (original MsC 37.2.30.3) from Charles
McGrath, outlining suggested changes in the text.

MUNRO, ALICE, 1931-   MsC 37.11.10
   Who do you think you are? : Simon's luck : short
   story fragments, n.d.

   7 items : 17 p.
   Typescript with holograph revisions. Untitled
   fragments, possibly related to Sheila section in
   four-part Emily ; Sheila ; Angela version of Simon's
   luck. (Only Emily section included in published
   version.)

MUNRO, ALICE, 1931-   MsC 37.11.11
   Who do you think you are? : Simon's luck : short
   story fragments, n.d.

   3 items : 5 p.
   Typescript. Untitled fragments related to early
   versions of Simon's luck.

MUNRO, ALICE, 1931-   MsC 37.11.12
   Who do you think you are? : Simon's luck : short
   story fragments, n.d.

   4 items : 4 p.
   Typescript. Untitled beginning fragments, probably
   from early versions of Simon's luck.

MUNRO, ALICE, 1931-   MsC 37.11.13
   Who do you think you are? : Simon's luck : short
   story fragments, n.d.

   5 items : 11 p.
   Holograph, typescript and typescript with holograph
   revisions. Untitled fragments from several early
   drafts of Simon's luck. 1 p. holograph, 10 p.
   typescript.

MUNRO, ALICE, 1931–   MsC 37.11.14
    Who do you think you are? : Simon's luck : short
    story fragments, n.d.

    14 items : 34 p.
    Typescript and typescript with holograph revisions.
    Untitled. Fragments possibly consecutive, producing
    a complete draft.

MUNRO, ALICE, 1931–   MsC 37.11.15
    Who do you think you are? : Simon's luck : short
    story fragment, n.d.

    1 item : 2 p.
    Typescript with holograph revisions. Includes parts
    of sections I and II from a draft of the Emily ;
    Sheila ; Angela version of Simon's luck. Possibly
    part of same draft as MsC 37.11.16-17.

MUNRO, ALICE, 1931–   MsC 37.11.16
    Who do you think you are? : Simon's luck : short
    story fragment, n.d.

    1 item : 18 p. on 17 leaves.
    Typescript with holograph revisions. Includes part
    of section II and section III from a draft of the
    Emily ; Sheila ; Angela version of Simon's luck.
    Possibly from same draft as MsC 37.11.15 and
    MsC 37.11.17.

MUNRO, ALICE, 1931–   MsC 37.11.17
    Who do you think you are? : Simon's luck : short
    story fragment, n.d.

    1 item : 3 p.
    Typescript with holograph revisions. Part IV of a
    draft of the Emily ; Sheila ; Angela version of
    Simon's luck. Possibly from same draft as
    MsC 37.11.15-16.

MUNRO, ALICE, 1931–   MsC 37.11.18
Who do you think you are? : Simon's luck : short
story fragments, n.d.

3 items : 4 p.
Typescript with holograph and cut and paste
revisions. Probably originally part of MsC 37.11.19.

MUNRO, ALICE, 1931–   MsC 37.11.19
Who do you think you are? : Simon's luck : short
story fragment, n.d.

1 item : 12 p.
Typescript with holograph revisions. Untitled
fragment.

MUNRO, ALICE, 1931–   MsC 37.11.20
Who do you think you are? : Simon's luck : short
story, n.d.

1 item : 33 p.
Typescript with holograph revisions. Titled.
Signed "Alice Munro". Complete draft of the
four-part Emily ; Sheila ; Angela version of Simon's
luck.

MUNRO, ALICE, 1931–   MsC 37.11.21
Who do you think you are? : Simon's luck : short
story, n.d.

1 item : 33 p.
Typescript (photocopy) with holograph revisions.
Titled. Photocopy of MsC 37.11.20 after most
revisions made. Holograph annotation on verso of
p. 1. Emily ; Sheila ; Angela version of Simon's
luck.

MUNRO, ALICE, 1931–   MsC 37.11.22
   Who do you think you are? : Simon's luck, part I,
   Emily : short story, n.d.

   1 item : 15 p.
   Typescript (photocopy) with holograph revisions.
   Holograph and holograph (photocopy) title. Ending
   (p. 15) crossed out. Part I of the Emily ; Sheila ;
   Angela version of Simon's luck. (Original typescript
   in MsC 38.4.1.4.)

MUNRO, ALICE, 1931–   MsC 37.11.23
   Who do you think you are? : Simon's luck, part II,
   Sheila : short story, n.d.

   1 item : 11 p.
   Typescript with holograph revisions. Holograph title
   II Sheila. Original ending (see MsC 37.11.24)
   excised. Part II Of the Emily ; Sheila ; Angela
   version of Simon's luck.

MUNRO, ALICE, 1931–   MsC 37.11.24
   Who do you think you are? : Simon's luck, part II,
   Sheila : short story, n.d.

   1 item : 11 p.
   Typescript (photocopy) with holograph revisions.
   Holograph (photocopy) title II Sheila. Photocopy of
   MsC 37.11.23 before revisions and before ending
   excised. Part II of the Emily ; Sheila ; Angela
   version of Simon's luck.

MUNRO, ALICE, 1931–   MsC 37.11.25
   Who do you think you are? : Simon's luck, part II,
   Sheila : short story, n.d.

   1 item : 13 p.
   Holograph and typescript with holograph and cut and
   paste revisions. Holograph title II – Sheila.
   Probably a segment of the early four part Emily ;
   Sheila ; Angela version of Simon's luck. 4 p.
   holograph, 9 p. typescript.

MUNRO, ALICE, 1931–   MsC 37.11.26
    Who do you think you are? : Simon's luck, part III,
    Angela : short story fragment, n.d.

    1 item : 12 p. on 11 leaves.
    Typescript (photocopy) with holograph revisions.
    Holograph (photocopy) title III - Angela. Page 6
    missing. Pages 11-12 ending is a photocopy of p. 2
    of MsC 37.11.27; original typescript for remainder of
    draft (p. 1-10) in MsC 38.4.1.4. Part III of the
    Emily ; Sheila ; Angela version of Simon's luck.

MUNRO, ALICE, 1931–   MsC 37.11.27
    Who do you think you are? : Simon's luck,
    part IV : short story, n.d.

    1 item : 2 p.
    Typescript with holograph and cut and paste
    revisions. Conclusion (part IV) of the Emily ;
    Sheila ; Angela version of Simon's luck. Probably
    made up of endings excised from MsC 37.11.23 and
    from the original typescript of MsC 37.11.22 and
    MsC 37.11.26.

MUNRO, ALICE, 1931–   MsC 37.11.28
    Who do you think you are? : Spelling : short story
    fragment, n.d.

    1 item : 3 p.
    Typescript with holograph revisions. Untitled
    fragment, possibly related to early versions of
    Spelling.

MUNRO, ALICE, 1931–   MsC 37.11.29
    Who do you think you are? : Spelling : short story
    fragments, n.d.

    3 items : 8 p. on 5 leaves.
    Holograph, typescript and typescript with holograph
    revisions. Untitled fragments, possibly related to
    early versions of Spelling. Unrelated holograph text
    on verso of fragment 2 similar to unpublished photo
    album text titled Suicide corners. 4 p. holograph,
    4 p. typescript.

MUNRO, ALICE, 1931–   MsC 37.11.30
    Who do you think you are? : Spelling : short story
    fragments, n.d.

    6 items : 14 p.
    Typescript and typescript with holograph revisions.
    Untitled fragments probably related to Spelling.
    Segments of fragment 1 similar to material in Royal
    beatings. Some fragments possibly consecutive.

MUNRO, ALICE, 1931–   MsC 37.11.31
    Who do you think you are? : Spelling : short story
    fragments, n.d.

    3 items : 10 p.
    Typescript with holograph revisions. Untitled
    fragments related to Spelling. Fragments also
    include material similar to sections of Royal beatings,
    Half a grapefruit and Characters.

MUNRO, ALICE, 1931–   MsC 37.11.32
    Who do you think you are? : Spelling : short story
    fragments, n.d.

    6 items : 19 p.
    Typescript and typescript with holograph revisions.
    Untitled fragments from various drafts of Spelling.

MUNRO, ALICE, 1931–   MsC 37.11.33
    Who do you think you are? : Spelling : short story
    fragments, n.d.

    2 items : 5 p.
    Typescript with holograph revisions. Untitled
    fragments.

MUNRO, ALICE, 1931–   MsC 37.11.34
Who do you think you are? : Spelling : short story
fragment, n.d.

1 item : 7 p.
Typescript. Untitled.

MUNRO, ALICE, 1931–   MsC 37.11.35
Who do you think you are? : Spelling : short story,
n.d.

1 item : 14 p.
Typescript (photocopy) with holograph revisions.
Titled. Signed "Alice Munro". Title page includes
holograph annotations "1st version", "Virginia
Barber" and New York address. Virginia Barber
label on verso of last page.

MUNRO, ALICE, 1931–   MsC 37.11.36
Who do you think you are? : Spelling : short story,
n.d.

1 item : 14 p.
Typescript (photocopy) with holograph revisions.
Reduced photocopy of MsC 37.11.34. Includes
holograph (photocopy) signature "Alice Munro",
annotation "Virginia Barber" and New York address.

MUNRO, ALICE, 1931–   MsC 37.11.37
Who do you think you are? : Spelling : short story,
n.d.

1 item : 13 p.
Typescript with holograph revisions. Titled.
Signed "Alice Munro". Title page includes holograph
annotation "2nd version". Includes photocopy of the
item. 13 p. typescript (photocopy).

MUNRO, ALICE, 1931–   MsC 37.11.38
   Who do you think you are? : Spelling : short story
   fragments, n.d.

   5 items : 16 p.
   Typescript and typescript with holograph revisions.
   First item titled. Fragments possibly from one
   draft; order of fragments may not be as filed.

MUNRO, ALICE, 1931–   MsC 37.11.39
   Who do you think you are? : Spelling : short story,
   n.d.

   1 item : 7 p.
   Typescript (photocopy). Holograph (photocopy) title
   and signature "Alice Munro". Complete(?).

MUNRO, ALICE, 1931–   MsC 37.12.1
   Who do you think you are? : Spelling : short story,
   n.d.

   1 item : 16 p. on 15 leaves.
   Typescript with holograph and cut and paste
   revisions. Untitled. Probably a revised clean copy
   of MsC 37.12.25. Order of pages may not be as
   filed.

MUNRO, ALICE, 1931–   MsC 37.12.2-3
   Who do you think you are? : Spelling : short story,
   n.d.

   1 item : 15 p.
   Typescript (photocopy) with holograph revisions.
   Titled. Signed "by Alice Munro". Photocopy of
   MsC 37.12.1 before cut and paste and other
   revisions. Includes attached holograph annotation
   "other versions of stories". MsC 37.12.3 is a
   photocopy of MsC 37.12.2; includes attached
   holograph annotation "older version". 15 p.
   typescript (photocopy).

MUNRO, ALICE, 1931–   MsC 37.12.4
Who do you think you are? : Spelling : short story,
n.d.

1 item : 17 p.
Typescript with holograph revisions (photocopy).
Holograph (photocopy) title.

MUNRO, ALICE, 1931–   MsC 37.12.5
Who do you think you are? : Spelling : short story,
n.d.

1 item : 21 p.
Typescript. Titled. Clean copy of MsC 37.12.4
with a revision from third to first person for Rose.

MUNRO, ALICE, 1931–   MsC 37.12.6
Spelling : page proofs, 1978 June.

1 item : 3 p.
Author's page proofs (photocopy) from Weekend
Magazine. Holograph revision on third page.
Holograph title, date and pagination. Includes
repository photocopy of covering letter (original
MsC 37.2.49) from Weekend Magazine. (Published in
Weekend Magazine, v. 28, no. 24, June 17, 1978.)

MUNRO, ALICE, 1931–   MsC 37.12.7
Who do you think you are? : Who do you think you
are? : short story fragment, n.d.

1 item : 13 p.
Holograph. Untitled.

MUNRO, ALICE, 1931–   MsC 37.12.8
Who do you think you are? : Who do you think you
are? : short story, n.d.

1 item : 16 p. on 15 leaves.
Typescript. Titled.

MUNRO, ALICE, 1931–   MsC 37.12.9
    Who do you think you are? : Who do you think you
    are? : short story fragments, n.d.

    4 items : 11 p.
    Typescript and typescript with holograph revisions.
    Untitled fragments from more than one draft.

MUNRO, ALICE, 1931–   MsC 37.12.10
    Who do you think you are? : Who do you think you
    are? : short story, n.d.

    1 item : 15 p.
    Typescript with holograph revisions.   Titled.

MUNRO, ALICE, 1931–   MsC 37.12.11
    Who do you think you are? : Who do you think you
    are? : short story fragment, n.d.

    1 item : 10 p. on 5 leaves.
    Holograph and typescript (photocopy) with holograph
    additions.   Untitled fragment.   Typescript pages are
    photocopies of pages in MsC 37.12.10.   5 p.
    holograph, 5 p. typescript.

MUNRO, ALICE, 1931–   MsC 37.12.12
    Who do you think you are? : Wild swans : short
    story fragments, n.d.

    3 items : 8 p.
    Holograph, typescript and typescript with holograph
    revisions.   Untitled fragments with sections related
    to Wild swans, The beggar maid and Sunday
    afternoon.   4 p. holograph, 4 p. typescript.

MUNRO, ALICE, 1931–   MsC 37.12.13
Who do you think you are? : Wild swans : short
story fragment, n.d.

1 item : 3 p. on 2 leaves.
Holograph and typescript. Untitled fragment with
section related to Wild swans. 1 p. holograph, 2 p.
typescript.

MUNRO, ALICE, 1931–   MsC 37.12.14
Who do you think you are? : Wild swans : short
story, n.d.

1 item : 5 p. on 4 leaves.
Typescript with holograph revisions. Untitled.
Similar to section of Wild swans. Holograph
annotation "Train" on verso of last page.

MUNRO, ALICE, 1931–   MsC 37.12.15
Who do you think you are? : Wild swans : short
story fragment, n.d.

1 item : 7 p.
Typescript with holograph revisions. Untitled.

MUNRO, ALICE, 1931–   MsC 37.12.16
Who do you think you are? : Wild swans : short
story, n.d.

1 item : 8 p.
Typescript. Untitled.

MUNRO, ALICE, 1931–   MsC 37.12.17
Who do you think you are? : Wild swans : short
story, n.d.

1 item : 10 p.
Typescript with holograph revisions. Titled.

MUNRO, ALICE, 1931–
    Who do you think you are? : Wild swans : short
    story, 1977(?).

    1 item : 10 p.
    Typescript (photocopy). Photocopy of MsC 37.12.17
    before revisions. Virginia Barber label on first
    page. Includes repository photocopy of covering
    letter (original MsC 37.2.47.9), dated March 31,
    1977, from Virginia Barber, indicating that the draft
    had been forwarded from that agency.

MsC 37.12.18

MUNRO, ALICE, 1931–
    Who do you think you are? : Wild swans : short
    story, n.d.

    1 item : 10 p.
    Typescript with holograph revisions. Titled. Clean
    copy of MsC 37.12.17.

MsC 37.12.19

MUNRO, ALICE, 1931–
    Wild swans : galleys, 1977(?).

    1 item : 4 p.
    Author's proof (photocopy). Copy edited. Page 1
    includes holograph annotation "Author". Probably
    from Toronto Life. (Enclosed repository photocopy
    of letter from Toronto Life possibly accompanied
    galleys. Original letter in MsC 37.2.40.2. Wild
    swans published in Toronto Life, April 1978.)

MsC 37.12.20

MUNRO, ALICE, 1931–
    Who do you think you are? : Wild swans : short
    story, n.d.

    1 item : 13 p.
    Typescript (photocopy) and typescript with
    holograph revisions. Titled. Clean copy of the
    draft of Wild swans (p. 59–67) in short story
    collection manuscript of Who do you think you are?
    in MsC 37.12.24. Pages 1–12 typescript
    (photocopy); p. l3 missing; p. 14 typescript.

MsC 37.12.21

MUNRO, ALICE, 1931–   MsC 37.12.22
Who do you think you are? : Wild swans : short
story fragment, n.d.

1 item : 1 p.
Typescript. Variant ending. Holograph pagination
and title annotation.

MUNRO, ALICE, 1931–   MsC 37.12.23
Who do you think you are? : preparatory work, n.d.

3 items : 5 p.
Holograph. Includes chronological list of stories,
list of names and brief outlines for a number of
short stories. One outline titled Places at home
related to short story collection Who do you think
you are?.

MUNRO, ALICE, 1931–   MsC 37.12.24
Who do you think you are? : short stories, n.d.

1 item : 146 p. on 141 leaves.
Typescript with holograph revisions; p. 123, 131
typescript (photocopy); p. 150 cut and paste
revision; p. 1, 122 missing. Stories originally
found separately in A. Munro's papers; manuscript
arrangement based on pagination in upper right hand
corner. Manuscript probably later dismantled, with
major revisions made to some stories. Missing p. 23,
38–39, 57–58, 68–69, 100–101, 133–134 and 153–154
had been pulled and reorganized to produce a draft
of Spelling (see following file MsC 37.12.25).
Holograph annotations on title pages of The beggar
maid, Mischief and Providence indicate revised
character names. A. Munro's holograph note
attached to p. 116 regarding change in text.

MUNRO, ALICE, 1931–   MsC 37.12.25
Who do you think you are? : Spelling : short story,
n.d.

1 item : 13 p.
Typescript with holograph revisions. Holograph
title. Stroked out pagination indicates story
originally part of manuscript of collection Who do you
think you are? in the preceding file (MsC 37.12.24).

MUNRO, ALICE, 1931–   MsC 37.12.26
    Who do you think you are? : Spelling : short story
    fragment, n.d.

    1 item : 2 p.
    Typescript. Untitled fragment, probably originally
    part of MsC 37.12.25. (See photocopy draft of
    Spelling in MsC 37.12.29 for confirmation.)

MUNRO, ALICE, 1931–   MsC 37.12.27
    Who do you think you are? : Mischief : short story
    fragments, n.d.

    2 items : 2 p.
    Typescript and typescript with revision. Untitled
    fragments, probably original typescript for p. 123,
    131 of Mischief in collection manuscript
    MsC 37.12.24.

MUNRO, ALICE, 1931–   MsC 37.12.28
    Who do you think you are? : Providence : short
    story fragments, n.d.

    3 items : 5 p.
    Typescript and typescript with holograph revisions.
    First fragment titled. Fragments possibly originally
    part of Providence (p. 135, 141, 150–152) in
    MsC 37.12.24.

MUNRO, ALICE 1931–   Msc 37.12.29
Who do you think you are? : short stories, n.d.

1 item : 128 p.
Typescript (photocopy); p. 126 typescript; p. 8-9
cut and paste revisions; missing p. 1, 64-65.
Stories originally found separately in A. Munro's
papers; partial manuscript arrangement based on
pagination in upper left hand corner. With the
exception of Spelling, stories are photocopies of
those in MsC 37.12.24 before revisions. Spelling
(p. 2-13) is a rearranged photocopy of
MsC 37.12.25, except for p. 8-9, which vary.
Variant beginning for Half a grapefruit (includes
holograph title and A. Munro's signature) lacks
collection pagination and was possibly added later.
Leaf between p. 3 and 4 also lacks collection pagination.
Manuscript for Mischief incomplete. See following
file for manuscript of Providence which is also
possibly part of this collected short story
manuscript.

MUNRO, ALICE, 1931–   Msc 37.12.30
Who do you think you are? : Providence : short
story, n.d.

1 item : 18 p. on 17 leaves.
Typescript and typescript (photocopy) with
holograph revisions; p. 7 cut and paste. Original
typescript in MsC 37.12.24 and 37.12.28. Pagination
in upper left corner (p. 136-152) indicates material
is possibly part of the collected short story
manuscript of Who do you think you are? in the
preceding file. (NOTE: Material in this file was
originally part of the second A. Munro accession
(MsC 38), but was moved to the first accession to
consolidate this collected short story manuscript.)

MUNRO, ALICE, 1931–   Msc 37.13.1
Who do you think you are? : short stories, n.d.

1 item : 60 p. on 58 leaves.
Typescript (photocopy) with holograph revisions;
p. 59-60 typescript; p. 25, 41-44 holograph; p. 24,
40 cut and paste with holograph additions. Stories
originally found separately in A. Munro's papers;
partial manuscript arrangement based on pagination.
Text is a photocopy of material in MsC 37.12.29 after
some revisions were made and story titles were
stroked out. Material in the following three files is
possibly part of this collection manuscript.

MUNRO, ALICE, 1931–   MsC 37.13.2
Who do you think you are? : short story fragments,
n.d.

2 items : 4 p.
Typescript (photocopy), holograph and typescript
(photocopy) with holograph revisions. Typescript
(photocopy) text copied from Spelling (p. 5-6) in
collection manuscript MsC 37.12.29. Fragments
possibly follow consecutively material in preceding
file (MsC 37.13.1), pagination unclear. 2 p.
holograph, 2 p. typescript.

MUNRO, ALICE, 1931–   MsC 37.13.3
Who do you think you are? : short stories, n.d.

1 item : 90 p. on 87 leaves.
Typescript (photocopy) with holograph revisions and
additions. Stories originally found separately in
A. Munro's papers; manuscript arrangement based on
stroked out titles and continuous pagination in upper
left hand corners. Material is possibly consecutive
to MsC 37.13.1-2, a partial manuscript of Who do
you think you are?. Pages 66-128 (upper left
pagination) and part of p. 135 are photocopies of
stories in MsC 37.12.29 with titles and pagination
stroked out; draft from which p. 129-152 were
copied is missing. Most of the original typescript is
in MsC 37.12.24 and MsC 37.12.28.

MUNRO, ALICE, 1931–   MsC 37.13.4
Who do you think you are? : Spelling : short story
fragment, n.d.

1 item : 9 p. on 8 leaves.
Typescript (photocopy) with holograph additions and
revisions; third page is a cut and paste revision.
Photocopy of Spelling in MsC 37.12.29 with title and
pagination stroked out. Missing pages (part of p.
3, p. 5-6, 10-11) are incorporated in MsC 37.13.1-2.
Material possibly part of manuscript of Who do you
think you are? (see three preceding files).
Arrangement of pages may not be as filed, and
position in collection manuscript is unknown.

MUNRO, ALICE, 1931-   MsC 37.13.5
Who do you think you are? : short stories, n.d.

1 item : 61 p.
Typescript (photocopy) with holograph revisions.
Possibly a partial manuscript (p. II4-124, 127-176)
of short story collection Who do you think you are?.
Consists of Emily ; Sheila ; Angela version of
Simon's luck. (NOTE: Subsequent to the above
description being made, material in this file was
found to be part of a collected short story
manuscript of Who do you think you are? in the
second A. Munro accession (MsC 38). In order to
consolidate the collection manuscript, material in this
file has been moved to MsC 38.4.3 in the second
A. Munro accession.)

MUNRO, ALICE, 1931-   MsC 37.13.6
Who do you think you are? : Spelling : short story,
n.d.

1 item : 23 p.
Typescript with holograph revisions. Pagination (p.
243-265) suggests story is part of the same collection
manuscript as preceding file. (NOTE: Subsequent
to the above description being made, material in this
file was found to be part of a collected short story
manuscript of Who do you think you are? in the
second A. Munro accession (MsC 38). In order to
consolidate the collection manuscript, material in this
file has been moved to MsC 38.4.4 in the second
A. Munro accession.)

MUNRO, ALICE, 1931-   MsC 37.13.7
Photo album text : list of titles, n.d.

1 item : 1 p.
Holograph list of titles, probably for untitled work
intended as text for Peter D'Angelo's Ontario photo
album. A. Munro had not seen the photo album,
and the text was unpublished. Text also related to
material in the short story collection Who do you
think you are?.

MUNRO, ALICE, 1931–   MsC 37.13.8
   Photo album text, n.d.

   2 items : 11 p. on 9 leaves.
   Typescript and holograph. Possibly related to text
   intended for Peter D'Angelo's Ontario photo album.
   Material also related to Characters and to stories in
   collection Who do you think you are?. Holograph
   fragment in item 2 related to titled fragments The
   war hero, the boy murderer, the lady ventriloquist.
   2 p. holograph, 9 p. typescript.

MUNRO, ALICE, 1931–   MsC 37.13.9
   Photo album text, n.d.

   12 items : 18 p.
   Typescript and typescript with holograph revisions.
   Holograph annotations "Rose", "Boy M" and "Father"
   on verso of three pages. Material probably written
   as text for P. D'Angelo's Ontario photo album, but
   not included in paginated versions in
   MsC 37.13.12-13. Includes eight titled short
   descriptive pieces or stories (three titles have two
   versions). Some material also related to stories in
   the collection Who do you think you are?.

MUNRO, ALICE, 1931–   MsC 37.13.10
   Photo album text, n.d.

   23 items : 47 p.
   Typescript and typescript (photocopy) with
   holograph revisions. Includes twenty-three titled
   short descriptive pieces or stories (first story has
   three copies) intended as text for Peter D'Angelo's
   Ontario photo album. Text unpublished. Holograph
   story outline on verso of second page in fragment 2.
   Material arranged according to paginated version
   (MsC 37.13.13); original order may not be as filed.
   Some of the text also related to Characters, The war
   hero, the boy murderer, the lady ventriloquist and
   particularly to stories in the collection Who do you
   think you are?.

MUNRO, ALICE, 1931–   MsC 37.13.11
    Photo album text, n.d.

        1 item : 28 p.
        Typescript with holograph revisions. Holograph
        annotation "The Mad Steer" on verso of p. 26.
        Includes twenty-two titled short descriptive pieces or
        stories intended for Peter D'Angelo's Ontario photo
        album. Text unpublished. Material arranged
        according to paginated version (MsC 37.13.12);
        original order may not be as filed. Some of the
        material also related to Characters, The war hero,
        the boy murderer, the lady ventriloquist and
        particularly to stories in the collection Who do you
        think you are?.

MUNRO, ALICE, 1931–   MsC 37.13.12
    Photo album text, n.d.

        1 item : 28 p.
        Typescript (photocopy) with holograph additions and
        revisions. Paginated. Photocopy of material in
        MsC 37.13.11 before holograph addition. Includes
        twenty-three titled short descriptive pieces or
        stories intended for Peter D'Angelo's Ontario photo
        album. Text unpublished. Some of the material also
        related to Characters, The war hero, the boy
        murderer, the lady ventriloquist and particularly to
        stories in the collection Who do you think you are?.

MUNRO, ALICE, 1931–   MsC 37.13.13
    Photo album text, n.d.

        1 item : 32 p.
        Typescript and typescript (photocopy) with
        holograph revisions. Pages 1-3, 31 typescript;
        p. 4-30 and variant p. 31 are photocopies of material
        in MsC 37.13.11. Manuscript arrangement based on
        pagination. Includes twenty-five titled short
        descriptive pieces or stories for Peter D'Angelo's
        Ontario photo album. Text unpublished. Some of
        the material also related to Characters, The war
        hero, the boy murderer, the lady ventriloquist and
        particularly to stories in the collection Who do you
        think you are?.

MUNRO, ALICE, 1931–   MsC 37.13.14
    Photo album text, n.d.

    1 item : 3 p.
    Typescript (photocopy). Photocopy of p. 1-3 in
    MsC 37.13.13. Fragment includes three titled short
    descriptive pieces or stories for Peter D'Angelo's
    Ontario photo album. Text unpublished.

MUNRO, ALICE, 1931–   MsC 37.13.15
    The moons of Jupiter : Accident : short story
    fragments, n.d.

    2 items : 10 p.
    Typescript and typescript with holograph revisions.
    Untitled fragments, possibly related to early versions
    of Accident.

MUNRO, ALICE, 1931–   MsC 37.13.16
    The moons of Jupiter : Accident : short story
    fragment, n.d.

    1 item : 5 p.
    Typescript. Untitled fragment, possibly related to
    early versions of Accident.

MUNRO, ALICE, 1931–   MsC 37.13.17
    The moons of Jupiter : Accident : short story
    fragment, n.d.

    1 item : 2 p.
    Typescript. Untitled fragment, possibly related to
    early versions of Accident.

MUNRO, ALICE, 1931–   MsC 37.13.18
    The moons of Jupiter : Accident : short story
    fragments, n.d.

    2 items : 3 p.
    Typescript and typescript with holograph revisions.
    Untitled fragments, possibly originally part of
    MsC 37.13.19.

MUNRO, ALICE, 1931–   MsC 37.13.19
The moons of Jupiter : Accident : short story, n.d.

1 item : 21 p. on 17 leaves.
Typescript with holograph revisions. Untitled.
Versos of several pages include short phrases of
holograph text. Verso of p. 14 includes a holograph
list of words, possibly related to collection Who do
you think you are?. Complete(?).

MUNRO, ALICE, 1931–   MsC 37.13.20
The moons of Jupiter : Accident : short story
fragment, n.d.

1 item : 1 p.
Typescript fragment possibly originally part of
MsC 37.13.21.

MUNRO, ALICE, 1931–   MsC 37.13.21
The moons of Jupiter : Accident : short story, n.d.

1 item : 27 p. on 26 leaves.
Typescript with holograph revisions. Holograph title
The accident, later published as Accident.

MUNRO, ALICE, 1931–   MsC 37.13.22
The moons of Jupiter : Accident : short story
fragment, n.d.

1 item : 2 p.
Typescript. Untitled beginning fragment similar to
beginning of MsC 37.13.23.

MUNRO, ALICE, 1931–   MsC 37.13.23-24
The moons of Jupiter : Accident : short story, n.d.

1 item : 31 p.
Typescript with holograph revisions. Titled.
MsC 37.13.24 is a copy of MsC 37.13.23. 31 p.
typescript (photocopy).

MUNRO, ALICE, 1931–   MsC 37.13.25
    The moons of Jupiter : Accident : short story,
    1977(?).

    1 item : 31 p.
    Typescript (photocopy). Titled. Signed
    "A. Munro". Photocopy of MsC 37.13.23. Includes
    repository photocopy of covering letter (1977 June
    13), from Virginia Barber relating that Cosmopolitan
    has rejected Accident and that this "older version"
    is being returned to A. Munro. (Original letter in
    MsC 37.2.47.12.)

MUNRO, ALICE, 1931–   MsC 37.13.26
    The moons of Jupiter : Accident : short story, n.d.

    1 item : 30 p.
    Typescript with holograph revisions. Titled.
    Signed "Alice Munro".

MUNRO, ALICE, 1931–   MsC 37.13.27
    The moons of Jupiter : Accident : short story
    fragment, n.d.

    1 item : 27 p.
    Typescript (photocopy) with holograph revisions.
    Photocopy of p. 4-30 of MsC 37.13.26. Verso of last
    page contains holograph lists of page counts(?) and
    titles, possibly indicating that Accident and
    Chaddeleys and Flemings were being considered for a
    collection also including most of the short stories in
    Who do you think you are?.

MUNRO, ALICE, 1931–   MsC 37.13.28
    Accident : author's proof, 1977(?).

    1 item : 16 p.
    Typescript (photocopy) author's proof from Toronto
    Life. Copy edited; holograph revisions by
    A. Munro. Includes repository photocopy of
    covering letter (1977 September 23), from Toronto
    Life indicating that Accident will be published in
    the November 1977 issue. (Original letter in
    MsC 37.2.40.1.)

MUNRO, ALICE, 1931–   MsC 37.14.1
    The moons of Jupiter : Chaddeleys and
    Flemings : short story, n.d.

    1 item : 22 p.
    Typescript with holograph revisions. Untitled.
    Early version of Chaddeleys and Flemings. Includes
    material from both Connection and The stone in the
    field, although not divided into parts nor subtitled.

MUNRO, ALICE, 1931–   MsC 37.14.2
    The moons of Jupiter : Chaddeleys and
    Flemings : short story fragments, n.d.

    4 items : 5 p.
    Typescript and typescript with holograph revisions.
    Untitled fragments from unidentified drafts.

MUNRO, ALICE, 1931–   MsC 37.14.3
    The moons of Jupiter : Ancestors : short story
    fragment, n.d.

    1 item : 16 p.
    Typescript with holograph revisions. Titled
    Ancestors, later published in The moons of Jupiter
    as Chaddeleys and Flemings. Includes material from
    Connection and The stone in the field, although not
    divided into parts nor subtitled.

MUNRO, ALICE, 1931–   MsC 37.14.4
    The moons of Jupiter : Chaddeleys and
    Flemings : short story fragment, n.d.

    1 item : 1 p.
    Holograph ending fragment for The stone in the field
    section of Chaddeleys and Flemings.

MUNRO, ALICE, 1931–   Msc 37.14.5
    The moons of Jupiter : Chaddeleys and
    Flemings : short story fragment, n.d.

    1 item : 2 p. on 1 leaf.
    Typescript with holograph revisions; holograph
    addition on verso. Original typescript from which
    p. 16 in MsC 37.14.7 was copied. From the section
    later titled The stone in the field. (NOTE:
    Subsequent to the above description being .made,
    material in this file was found to be part of a
    manuscript for Chaddeleys and Flemings in the
    second A. Munro accession (MsC 38). In order to
    complete the manuscript, material in this file has
    been moved to MsC 38.8.12 in the second A. Munro
    accession.)

MUNRO, ALICE, 1931–   Msc 37.14.6
    The moons of Jupiter : Chaddeleys and
    Flemings : short story fragment, n.d.

    1 item : 1 p.
    Typescript with holograph revisions. Ending
    fragment, possibly for MsC 37.14.7 or original
    typescript in MsC 38.8.12. Includes A. Munro's
    holograph annotation "Marianne – Here is a new last
    page (instead of the one you have)". Part of the
    section later titled The stone in the field.

MUNRO, ALICE, 1931–   Msc 37.14.7
    The moons of Jupiter : Chaddeleys and
    Flemings : short story, n.d.

    1 item : 26 p. on 25 leaves.
    Typescript (photocopy) with holograph revisions.
    Titled. Includes material from sections Connections
    and. The stone in the field, although not divided into
    parts or subtitled. (Original typescript from which
    this item was copied is in MsC 38.8.12 in the second
    A. Munro accession.)

MUNRO, ALICE, 1931–   MsC 37.14.8
  The moons of Jupiter : The moons of Jupiter : short
  story fragment, n.d.

  1 item : 11 p.
  Typescript with holograph revisions. Untitled.
  Sections similar to material later published in
  Chaddeleys and Flemings, part II, The stone in the
  field.

MUNRO, ALICE, 1931–   MsC 37.14.9
  The moons of Jupiter : The moons of Jupiter : short
  story, n.d.

  1 item : 15 p.
  Typescript. Untitled. Complete(?).

MUNRO, ALICE, 1931–   MsC 37.14.10
  The moons of Jupiter : The moons of Jupiter : short
  story, n.d.

  1 item : 19 p.
  Typescript with holograph revisions. Untitled.
  Complete(?).

MUNRO, ALICE, 1931–   MsC 37.14.11
  The moons of Jupiter : The moons of Jupiter : short
  story, n.d.

  1 item : 19 p.
  Typescript with holograph revisions. Titled.

MUNRO, ALICE, 1931–   MsC 37.14.12
  The moons of Jupiter : The moons of Jupiter : short
  story fragment, n.d.

  1 item : 1 p.
  Typescript variant ending.

MUNRO, ALICE, 1931–   MsC 37.14.13
    The moons of Jupiter : Taking chances : short
    story, n.d.

    1 item : 21 p.
    Typescript (photocopy). Titled Taking chances,
    later published as The moons of Jupiter.

MUNRO, ALICE, 1931–   MsC 37.14.14
    The moons of Jupiter : The moons of Jupiter : short
    story, n.d.

    1 item : 21 p.
    Typescript (photocopy). Copy edited.
    MsC 37.14.13 and MsC 37.14.14 are photocopies of
    same unidentified draft. Title Taking chances
    revised to The moons of Jupiter. A. Munro's
    signature on title page stroked out; holograph
    annotation "Alice Munro" on last page. Probably
    edited for the New Yorker. (The moons of Jupiter
    published in the New Yorker, May 22, 1978.
    Another copy edited draft from the New Yorker in
    MsC 38.9.17.)

MUNRO, ALICE, 1931–   MsC 37.14.15–
UNCOLLECTED SHORT STORY SERIES, CA. 1950-197-.   37.16.34

302 ITEMS.
CONSISTS OF PUBLISHED SHORT STORIES NOT
INCLUDED IN COLLECTIONS DANCE OF THE HAPPY
SHADES, SOMETHING I'VE BEEN MEANING TO TELL
YOU, WHO DO YOU THINK YOU ARE? OR THE MOONS
OF JUPITER; UNPUBLISHED SHORT STORIES; AND
TITLED SHORT STORY FRAGMENTS. MANUSCRIPTS
ARRANGED ALPHABETICALLY BY TITLE; RELATED
UNTITLED FRAGMENTS FILED WITH RELEVANT TITLED
MATERIAL.

MUNRO, ALICE, 1931–   MsC 37.14.15
      Angie : short story fragment, n.d.

      1 item : 1 p.
      Holograph fragment.

MUNRO, ALICE, 1931–   MsC 37.14.16
      Another life : short story fragments, n.d.

      2 items : 9 p.
      Typescript with holograph revisions.   Holograph title
      on first item, second item untitled.

MUNRO, ALICE, 1931–   MsC 37.14.17
      The art of fiction : short story fragment, n.d.

      1 item : 1 p.
      Typescript.

MUNRO, ALICE, 1931–   MsC 37.14.18
      At the other place.
      p. 131-133.

      In the Canadian Forum, v. 35, no. 416, September
      1955. Author's name given as Alice Laidlaw, maiden
      name of A. Munro. Holograph deletion in text.

MUNRO, ALICE, 1931–   MsC 37.14.19
A basket of strawberries.
p. 32–33, 78–80, 82.

Detached from Mayfair, November 1953.

MUNRO, ALICE, 1931–   MsC 37.14.20
The boy murderer : short story fragments, n.d.

3 items : 6 p.
Typescript. First fragment titled. Items 1 and 2
possibly consecutive. Related material titled The
war hero, the boy murderer, the lady ventriloquist.

MUNRO, ALICE, 1931–   MsC 37.14.21
The boy murderer : short story fragments, n.d.

2 items : 20 p.
Typescript. Untitled fragments related to material in
the previous file titled The boy murderer. Other
related material titled The war hero, the boy
murderer, the lady ventriloquist.

MUNRO, ALICE, 1931–   MsC 37.14.22
The boy murderer : short story fragment, n.d.

1 item : 2 p.
Typescript. Titled. Related material titled The war
hero, the boy murderer, the lady ventriloquist.

MUNRO, ALICE, 1931–   MsC 37.14.23
The boy murderer : short story fragments, n.d.

17 items : 30 p.
Holograph and typescript. Untitled fragments, most
beginning "He (or Boyd) woke up with something
hurting him...". Similar to material in previous file
titled The boy murderer and related to material titled
The war hero, the boy murderer, the lady
ventriloquist. 1 p. holograph, 29 p. typescript.

MUNRO, ALICE, 1931–   MsC 37.14.24
    The boy murderer : short story fragments, n.d.

    4 items : 11 p.
    Typescript and typescript with holograph revisions.
    Untitled fragments beginning "Owen dreamt he was
    walking (going) down the road...". Similar to text
    in two preceding files and related to material titled
    The war hero, the boy murderer, the lady
    ventriloquist.

MUNRO, ALICE, 1931–   MsC 37.14.25
    The boy murderer : short story fragments, n.d.

    3 items : 7 p.
    Typescript. Untitled fragments beginning "Raymond
    woke up with something hurting him...". Similar
    material in three preceding files and related to
    material titled The war hero, the boy murderer, the
    lady ventriloquist.

MUNRO, ALICE, 1931–   MsC 37.14.26
    The boy murderer : short story fragment, n.d.

    1 item : 21 p.
    Typescript with holograph revisions. Untitled
    fragment similar to material in preceding files titled
    The boy murderer and to material titled The war
    hero, the boy murderer, the lady ventriloquist.
    Some segments related to novel Lives of girls and
    women, particularly chapters Princess Ida, Changes
    and ceremonies and Lives of girls and women.

MUNRO, ALICE, 1931–   MsC 37.14.27
    Certain moments in our history... : short story
    fragments, n.d.

    5 items : 22 p. on 21 leaves.
    Holograph, typescript and typescript with holograph
    revisions. Second fragment has holograph title;
    other fragments untitled. Item 1 is holograph story
    outline, possibly for Certain moments in our
    history.... Item 2 has sections related to Tell me
    yes or no. Unrelated line of text on verso of one
    page in item 2. 1 p. holograph, 21 p. typescript.

MUNRO, ALICE, 1931–   MsC 37.14.28
    Characters : short story outline, n.d.

    1 item : 1 p.
    Holograph.

MUNRO, ALICE, 1931–   MsC 37.14.29
    Characters : short story fragment, n.d.

    1 item : 13 p. on 11 leaves.
    Holograph and typescript with holograph revisions.
    Untitled. Includes sections rewritten and published
    in Half a grapefruit and Wild swans. Last section
    similar to material in Photo album text. Unrelated
    holograph text similar to parts of Spelling on verso
    of p. 1–2. Holograph diagrams and printing over
    text on two pages.

MUNRO, ALICE, 1931–   MsC 37.14.30
    Characters : short story fragments, n.d.

    2 items : 13 p.
    Typescript with holograph revisions. Untitled
    fragments, possibly consecutive, related to early
    versions of Characters. Includes sections similar to
    parts of Royal beatings, Half a grapefruit and Photo
    album text.

MUNRO, ALICE, 1931–   MsC 37.14.31
    Characters : short story fragments, n.d.

    2 items : 11 p. on 10 leaves.
    Holograph and typescript with holograph revisions.
    Untitled fragments, possibly consecutive. Includes
    sections rewritten and published in Half a
    grapefruit. 2 p. holograph, 9 p. typescript.

MUNRO, ALICE, 1931–   MsC 37.14.32
    Characters : short story fragments, n.d.

    6 items : 13 p.
    Typescript and typescript with holograph revisions.
    Untitled. Item 4 has sections related to Royal
    beatings and Half a grapefruit.

MUNRO, ALICE, 1931–   MsC 37.14.33
    Characters : short story fragments, n.d.

    7 items : 10 p.
    Holograph and typescript. Untitled miscellaneous
    fragments. Item 6 is photocopy of item 5. 2 p.
    holograph, 8 p. typescript.

MUNRO, ALICE, 1931–   MsC 37.14.34
    Pleistocene : short story, n.d.

    1 item : 17 p.
    Typescript with holograph revisions. Titled
    Pleistocene, later version published as Characters in
    Ploughshares, v. 4, no. 3, 1978. Includes section
    rewritten for Wild swans.

MUNRO, ALICE, 1931–   MsC 37.14.35
    Pleistocene : short story, n.d.

    1 item : 17 p.
    Typescript (photocopy). Photocopy of
    MsC 37.14.34. Title page has Virginia Barber label
    and A. Munro's holograph annotation "1st version".
    Titled Pleistocene, later version published as
    Characters in Ploughshares, v. 4, no. 3, 1978.
    Includes section rewritten for Wild swans.

MUNRO, ALICE, 1931–   MsC 37.14.36
    Pleistocene : short story, n.d.

    1 item : 16 p.
    Typescript. Titled Pleistocene, later version
    published as Characters. Includes p. 1, 10–11,
    13–14 from the first A. Munro accession (MsC 37);
    p. 2–9, 12, 15–16 found in second A. Munro
    accession (MsC 38) and relocated in this file to
    complete the draft. Rough copy of this draft in
    MsC 38.10.7. Section of the story rewritten as part
    of Wild swans.

MUNRO, ALICE, 1931–   MsC 37.14.37
    The cougar in the closet : short story fragment,
    n.d.

    1 item : 1 p.
    Typescript.

MUNRO, ALICE, 1931–   MsC 37.14.38
    The dancing bear : short story fragment, n.d.

    1 item : 4 p.
    Typescript with holograph revisions.

MUNRO, ALICE, 1931–   MsC 37.14.39
    The dangerous one.
    p. 49–51.

    Detached from Chatelaine, July 1957. Title The
    dangerous one stroked out and revised to The theft.
    Holograph revisions to text; holograph annotation
    "1957" on title page.

MUNRO, ALICE, 1931–   MsC 37.14.40
    Developing secrets : short story fragment, n.d.

    1 item : 2 p.
    Holograph.

MUNRO, ALICE, 1931-   MsC 37.14.41
    The dimensions of a shadow : short story fragment.
    p. 2-7.

    Photocopy of short story in Folio, v. 4, April 1950,
    published by University of Western Ontario. Pages
    8-9 missing. Poor quality copy. Author's name
    given as Alice Laidlaw, maiden name of A. Munro.
    Source of copy and date established by A. Munro.

MUNRO, ALICE, 1931-   MsC 37.14.42
    Dr. Needle : short story, n.d.

    1 item : 9 p. on 8 leaves.
    Typescript with holograph revisions. Holograph
    title. Story has some similarity to parts of Spelling.
    Complete(?). List of short story titles on verso of
    last page.

MUNRO, ALICE, 1931-   MsC 37.14.43
    Dr. Needle : short story fragments, n.d.

    2 items : 7 p.
    Typescript with holograph revisions. Holograph title
    on first item; second item untitled, possibly related
    to first fragment.

MUNRO, ALICE, 1931-   MsC 37.14.44
    The edge of town : short story fragment, n.d.

    1 item : 6 p. on 5 leaves.
    Typescript and holograph. Untitled. Includes
    p. 5-9, with unrelated(?) holograph text on verso of
    last page. Similar to published story titled The
    edge of town in the following file (MsC 37.14.45).

MUNRO, ALICE, 1931–   MsC 37.14.45
    The edge of town.
    p. 368-380.

    In Queen's Quarterly, v. 62, no. 3, Autumn 1955.
    Holograph revisions to text; holograph annotation
    "1955" on title page. Pages have been excised and
    are loose in periodical.

MUNRO, ALICE, 1931–   MsC 37.14.46
    Eternal springs : short story fragment, n.d.

    1 item : 3 p.
    Holograph.

MUNRO, ALICE, 1931–   MsC 37.15.1
    The funeral-goer : short story, ca. 1958-1959.

    1 item : 13 p.
    Typescript with holograph revisions.   Date
    established by A. Munro.

MUNRO, ALICE, 1931–   MsC 37.15.2
    Game laws : short story(?) fragment, n.d.

    1 item : 1 p.
    Typescript.   Crayon marking on verso.

MUNRO, ALICE, 1931–   MsC 37.15.3
    The girl murderer : short story fragments, n.d.

    2 items : 3 p.
    Typescript.   Holograph title on first fragment.
    Story similar to The boy murderer and The war
    hero, the boy murderer, the lady ventriloquist.

MUNRO, ALICE, 1931–   MsC 37.15.4
     The green April : short story, ca. 1953–1954.

     1 item : 6 p.
     Typescript with holograph revisions. Signed "Alice
     Munro". Title page includes holograph annotations
     "2.00–3.30" and "copies". Date established by
     A. Munro.

MUNRO, ALICE, 1931–   MsC 37.15.5
     The heart of an executioner : short story fragments,
     n.d.

     3 items : 8 p.
     Typescript. Three titled fragments. Not related to
     published story Executioners, sometimes also titled
     The heart of an executioner.

MUNRO, ALICE, 1931–   MsC 37.15.6
     The heart of an executioner : short story fragments,
     n.d.

     2 items : 6 p.
     Typescript with holograph correction. First
     fragment titled. Not related to published story
     Executioners, sometimes also titled The heart of an
     executioner. Fragments possibly consecutive.

MUNRO, ALICE, 1931–   MsC 37.15.7
     Home : short story fragments, n.d.

     3 items : 4 p.
     Typescript. First item titled. Fragments possibly
     from one draft.

MUNRO, ALICE, 1931–   MsC 37.15.8
    Home : short story fragment, n.d.

    1 item : 12 p.
    Holograph and typescript with holograph revisions.
    Untitled. Last three pages include short segments
    possibly out of sequence and an outline for end of
    story. 4 p. holograph, 8 p. typescript.

MUNRO, ALICE, 1931–   MsC 37.15.9
    Home : short story fragment, n.d.

    1 item : 8 p. on 7 leaves.
    Typescript with short holograph segment on verso of
    p. 3. Untitled.

MUNRO, ALICE, 1931–   MsC 37.15.10
    Home : short story fragments, n.d.

    2 items : 3 p.
    Typescript and typescript with holograph revisions.
    Untitled fragments.

MUNRO, ALICE, 1931–   MsC 37.15.11
    Home : short story, 1973 October.

    1 item : 22 p.
    Typescript (photocopy) with holograph revisions.
    Title Notes for a work has been revised by hand to
    Home. Page 22 includes A. Munro's holograph
    annotation "Oct 30, 1973   For John Metcalf with love
    Alice Munro". Date written established by
    A. Munro.

MUNRO, ALICE, 1931-   MsC 37.15.12
    Home : short story fragments, 1973 November.

    2 items : 4 p.
    Typescript (photocopy). Pages 18, 21-23 of draft
    very similar to published version in 74 : New
    Canadian stories, edited by David Helwig and Joan
    Harcourt. Includes A. Munro's holograph annotation
    on last page "for John Met[calf] Nov 12,". Date
    written established by A. Munro.

MUNRO, ALICE, 1931-   MsC 37.15.13
    A house on the beach : short story fragment, n.d.

    1 item : 4 p.
    Typescript.

MUNRO, ALICE, 1931-   MsC 37.15.14
    The house on the beach : short story, n.d.

    1 item : 8 p.
    Typescript. Complete(?). Similar story in
    MsC 37.15.I5-16 titled Houses.

MUNRO, ALICE, 1931-   MsC 37.15.15
    Houses : short story, n.d.

    1 item : 13 p. on 11 leaves.
    Typescript. Similar story in MsC 37.15.14 titled
    The house on the beach.

MUNRO, ALICE, 1931-   MsC 37.15.16
    Houses : short story fragment, n.d.

    1 item : 6 p.
    Typescript. Ending fragment. Similar story in
    previous file and in MsC 37.15.14 titled The
    house on the beach.

MUNRO, ALICE, 1931–   MsC 37.15.17
   How could I do that?.
   p. 16, 65-70.

   Detached from Chatelaine, March 1956. Title clipped
   from title page, and story retitled The chesterfield
   suite. Author's name given as Alice Laidlaw Munro.
   Holograph revisions to the text.

MUNRO, ALICE, 1931–   MsC 37.15.18
   Hur kunde jag?.
   p. 10-11, 26, 29, 33.

   In Vecko Revyn, no. 27, July 1956. Swedish
   version of How could I do that?. Author's name
   given as Alice Laidlaw Munro.

MUNRO, ALICE, 1931–   MsC 37.15.19
   I am the daughter to a river god : short story
   fragment, n.d.

   1 item : 3 p.
   Holograph. Untitled beginning fragment similar to
   fragments in MsC 37.15.21 titled I am the daughter
   of a river god.

MUNRO, ALICE, 1931–   MsC 37.15.20
   I am the daughter of a river god : short story
   fragments, n.d.

   6 items : 7 p.
   Typescript. Untitled fragments from several drafts,
   related to material in MsC 37.15.21 titled I am the
   daughter of a river god.

MUNRO, ALICE, 1931–   MsC 37.15.21
   I am the daughter of a river god : short story
   fragments, n.d.

   3 items : 9 p.
   Typescript. Items 1 and 3 titled; items 1 and 2
   possibly from same draft.

MUNRO, ALICE, 1931–   MsC 37.15.22
    I am the daughter of a river god : short story
    fragments, n.d.

    8 items : 28 p. on 27 leaves.
    Typescript. First fragment titled. Items 2 and 3
    possibly from same draft.

MUNRO, ALICE, 1931–   MsC 37.15.23
    I am the daughter of a river god : short story
    fragment, n.d.

    1 item : 2 p.
    Typescript with holograph revisions. Untitled
    fragment with sections similar to material titled I am
    the daughter of a river god.

MUNRO, ALICE, 1931–   MsC 37.15.24
    I am the daughter of a river god : short story
    fragments, n.d.

    2 items : 2 p.
    Holograph and typescript. First fragment titled.
    1 p. holograph, 1 p. typescript.

MUNRO, ALICE, 1931–   MsC 37.15.25
    The idyllic summer.
    p. 106-107, 109-110.

    In the Canadian Forum, August 1954. Author's name
    given as Alice Laidlaw Munro. Holograph deletion to
    text and annotation "1954" on title page. Pages
    have been excised and are loose in the periodical.

MUNRO, ALICE, 1931–   MsC 37.15.26
     Is she kind as she is fair? : short story fragments,
     n.d.

     6 items : 16 p. on 14 leaves.
     Typescript and typescript with holograph revisions.
     Untitled fragments about working at a summer hotel.
     Similar material in MsC 37.15.27 titled Is she kind as
     she is fair?. Last three fragments possibly from
     same draft.

MUNRO, ALICE, 1931–   MsC 37.15.27
     Is she kind as she is fair? : short story fragments,
     n.d.

     8 items : 9 p. on 8 leaves.
     Typescript. First fragment titled. Fragments about
     working at a summer hotel, all beginning "Between
     my first and second years at college...".

MUNRO, ALICE, 1931–   MsC 37.15.28
     Is she kind as she is fair? : short story fragment,
     n.d.

     1 item : 2 p.
     Typescript. Untitled fragment about working at a
     summer hotel. Similar to material in MsC 37.15.27
     titled Is she kind as she is fair?.

MUNRO, ALICE, 1931–   MsC 37.15.29
     Is she kind as she is fair? : short story fragment,
     n.d.

     1 item : 6 p. on 3 leaves.
     Typescript with holograph revisions. Untitled
     fragment about working at a summer hotel. Related
     material titled Is she kind as she is fair?. Text
     from different drafts on verso of p. 1–2.

MUNRO, ALICE, 1931–   MsC 37.15.30
Is she kind as she is fair? : short story fragments,
n.d.

9 items : 18 p.
Typescript and typescript with holograph revisions.
Untitled fragments about girls, usually Eva or Evie,
working at a summer hotel. Related material titled
Is she kind as she is fair?.

MUNRO, ALICE, 1931–   MsC 37.15.31
Is she kind as she is fair? : short story fragments,
n.d.

2 items : 6 p.
Typescript. Untitled fragments about working at a
summer hotel. Related material titled Is she kind as
she is fair?.

MUNRO, ALICE, 1931–   MsC 37.15.32
Is she kind as she is fair? : short story fragments,
n.d.

4 items : 9 p.
Typescript and typescript with holograph revisions.
Untitled fragments about working at a summer hotel.
Related material titled Is she kind as she is fair?.

MUNRO, ALICE, 1931–   MsC 37.15.33
Joanne : short story, n.d.

1 item : 22 p.
Typescript with holograph revisions. Untitled.
Similar to short story titled Joanne in the following
file (MsC 37.15.34).

MUNRO, ALICE, 1931–   MsC 37.15.34
Joanne : short story, n.d.

1 item : 21 p.
Typescript with holograph revisions (photocopy).
Holograph title.

MUNRO, ALICE, 1931–   MsC 37.15.35
    Joanne : short story fragments, n.d.

    7 items : 7 p.
    Holograph, typescript and typescript with holograph
    revisions.   Includes two variant p. 18s, five variant
    p. 21s.   Typescript sections of item 2 and item 3 are
    original text from which p. 18 and 21 in preceding
    file were copied.

MUNRO, ALICE, 1931–   MsC 37.15.36
    King Jupiter : short story fragments, n.d.

    2 items : 2 p.
    Typescript.

MUNRO, ALICE, 1931–   MsC 37.15.37
    The lady ventriloquist : short story fragment, n.d.

    1 item : 2 p.
    Typescript.   Holograph list of titles on verso of first
    page.

MUNRO, ALICE, 1931–   MsC 37.15.38
    Lemonade : short story fragment, n.d.

    1 item : 3 p.
    Typescript.   Holograph title.

MUNRO, ALICE, 1931–   MsC 37.15.39
    The liberation : short story, n.d.

    1 item : 9 p.
    Typescript with holograph deletions.   Signed "Alice
    Laidlaw", maiden name of A. Munro.

MUNRO, ALICE, 1931–   MsC 37.15.40
The foreigner : short story fragments, 1957.

2 items : 2 p.
Typescript. First fragment titled.   Similar material
titled Miss Posliff in following file.   Date established
by A. Munro.

MUNRO, ALICE, 1931–   MsC 37.15.41
Miss Posliff : short story fragment, 1957.

1 item : 12 p.
Typescript. Signed "Alice Munro".   Date established
by A. Munro.

MUNRO, ALICE, 1931–   MsC 37.15.42
My friend Irma : short story fragment, n.d.

1 item : 1 p.
Typescript.

MUNRO, ALICE, 1931–   MsC 37.15.43
The natural mistake : short story fragments, n.d.

2 items : 6 p.
Typescript.

MUNRO, ALICE, 1931–   MsC 37.15.44
Neighbourhood : short story fragment, n.d.

1 item : 3 p.
Typescript. Sections similar to material about the
"Musgrave house" in Walking on water and to parts
of chapter Heirs of the living body in Lives of girls
and women.

MUNRO, ALICE, 1931–   MsC 37.15.45
    Notes for Rapunzel : short story fragment, n.d.

    1 item : 1 p.
    Typescript.

MUNRO, ALICE, 1931–   MsC 37.15.46
    An offering for my enemy : short story fragment,
    n.d.

    1 item : 1 p.
    Typescript.

MUNRO, ALICE, 1931–   MsC 37.15.47
    On such a night : short story, 1959.

    1 item : 15 p.
    Typescript. Signed "Alice Munro". Date
    established as Summer 1959 by A. Munro.

MUNRO, ALICE, 1931–   MsC 37.15.48
    On such a night : short story fragment, n.d.

    1 item : 3 p.
    Typescript. Ending fragment, paginated p. 14-16.
    Material similar to that in preceding file
    (MsC 37.15.47).

MUNRO, ALICE, 1931–   MsC 37.15.49
    Parent-teacher interview : short story, n.d.

    1 item : 9 p.
    Typescript with holograph deletion. Similar to short
    story titled Parent-teacher interview in following
    file (MsC 37.15.50).

MUNRO, ALICE, 1931–   MsC 37.15.50
    Parent-teacher interview : short story, 1962.

    2 items : 12 p.
    Typescript. Titled. Signed "Anne Chamney",
    pseudonym of A. Munro. Item 2 is variant p. 9.
    Date established by A. Munro.

MUNRO, ALICE, 1931–   MsC 37.15.51
    Spring Saturday : short story fragment, 1953.

    1 item : 2 p.
    Typescript. Similar to story titled Pastime of a
    Saturday night in two following files. Date
    established by A. Munro.

MUNRO, ALICE, 1931–   MsC 37.15.52
    Pastime of a Saturday night : short story, 1953.

    1 item : 11 p.
    Typescript. Signed "Alice Laidlaw", maiden name of
    A. Munro. Date written established by A. Munro.
    Similar material titled Spring Saturday
    in MsC 37.15.51.

MUNRO, ALICE, 1931–   MsC 37.15.53
    Pastime of a Saturday night : short story, 1953.

    1 item : 10 p.
    Typescript with holograph deletions. Date written
    established by A. Munro. Similar material titled
    Spring Saturday in MsC 38.15.51.

MUNRO, ALICE, 1931–   MsC 37.15.54
    Places at home : short story fragments, n.d.

    2 items : 5 p. on 4 leaves.
    Typescript and typescript with holograph revisions.
    Descriptive fragments about Wawanash River and
    town of Jubilee (or Marnoch).

MUNRO, ALICE, 1931–   MsC 37.15.55
    A pound of cure : short story fragment, n.d.

    1 item : 2 p.
    Typescript. Not related to An ounce of cure.

MUNRO, ALICE, 1931–   MsC 37.16.1
    Rapunzel, Rapunzel : short story fragments, n.d.

    7 items : 13 p.
    Holograph and typescript. First fragment titled.
    Fragments 1 and 2 possibly consecutive; fragments
    3-6 probably from same draft and possibly
    consecutive. Beginning fragments all start "Ian
    Rickeby had read two books". 5 p. holograph, 8 p.
    typescript.

MUNRO, ALICE, 1931–   MsC 37.16.2
    Rapunzel, Rapunzel : short story fragments, n.d.

    4 items : 6 p.
    Typescript. Untitled fragments all beginning "I was
    in love with a boy who had read two books".
    Similar to story fragments titled Rapunzel, Rapunzel
    in preceding file (MsC 37.16.1).

MUNRO, ALICE, 1931–   MsC 37.16.3
    Rapunzel, Rapunzel : short story fragments, n.d.

    3 items : 6 p.
    Typescript. First fragment titled.

MUNRO, ALICE, 1931–   MsC 37.16.4
    Rapunzel, Rapunzel, let down thy gold hair : short
    story fragments, n.d.

    5 items : 9 p.
    Typescript and typescript with holograph revisions.
    Items 1-3 titled.

MUNRO, ALICE, 1931-   MsC 37.16.5
The return of the poet : short story, 1951.

1 item : 10 p.
Typescript (carbon copy). Date written established
as Summer 1951 by A. Munro.

MUNRO, ALICE, 1931-   MsC 37.16.6
The return of the poet : short story fragment, 1951.

1 item : 9 p.
Typescript (carbon copy). Copy of same draft as
preceding file; last page missing. Date written
established as Summer 1951 by A. Munro.

MUNRO, ALICE, 1931-   MsC 37.16.7
Simon and Elaine : short story fragments, n.d.

6 items : 13 p.
Typescript. Second fragment titled. Related to
material titled Simon and Elsie in following file.

MUNRO, ALICE, 1931-   MsC 37.16.8
Simon and Elsie : short story fragments, n.d.

3 items : 6 p.
Typescript. First fragment titled. Related to
material titled Simon and Elaine in preceding file;
sections also similar to parts of Simon's luck.

MUNRO, ALICE, 1931-   MsC 37.16.9
The strangers : short story fragment, 1951.

1 item : 2 p.
Typescript. Signed "Alice Laidlaw", maiden name of
A. Munro. Identified by A. Munro as having been
written Spring 1951 and as having been the first
story sold. (Sold to Robert Weaver of Canadian
Broadcasting Corporation.) Erased holograph
addition on p. 2.

MUNRO, ALICE, 1931–   MsC 37.16.10
     Suicide ladies : short story fragment, n.d.

     1 item : 11 p. on 10 leaves.
     Holograph and typescript with holograph revisions.
     Holograph title. Related material in notebook
     MsC 37.17.4. Story possibly related to "Rose"
     stories in Who do you think you are?. 10 p.
     holograph, 1 p. typescript.

MUNRO, ALICE, 1931–   MsC 37.16.11
     Suicide ladies : short story fragments, n.d.

     2 items : 8 p.
     Typescript. Untitled. Similar to material titled
     Suicide ladies in preceding file and in notebook
     MsC 37.17.4. Material possibly related to "Rose"
     stories in Who do you think you are?.

MUNRO, ALICE, 1931–   MsC 37.16.12
     Suicide ladies : short story fragment, n.d.

     1 item : 1 p.
     Typescript. Untitled. Possibly related to material
     titled Suicide ladies in the preceding file. Similar
     material also in text for Peter D'Angelo's photo album
     (MsC 37.13.7-14).

MUNRO, ALICE, 1931–   MsC 37.16.13
     Suicide ladies : short story fragment, n.d.

     1 items : 9 p.
     Typescript with holograph revisions. Untitled.
     Possibly related to material titled Suicide ladies and
     to "Rose" stories in Who do you think you are?.

MUNRO, ALICE, 1931–   MsC 37.16.14
     Three parties : short story fragments, n.d.

     2 items : 14 p.
     Holograph. Fragments possible from same draft.
     Sections similar to Simon's luck.

MUNRO, ALICE, 1931-   MsC 37.16.15
    Three parties : short story fragments, n.d.

    3 items : 19 p.
    Typescript with holograph revisions. Untitled
    fragments related to material titled Three parties in
    preceding file and with sections similar to Simon's
    luck.

MUNRO, ALICE, 1931-   MsC 37.16.16
    Three parties : short story fragments, n.d.

    2 items : 13 p.
    Typescript with holograph revision. Untitled.
    Related to material titled Three parties in preceding
    files. Sections similar to Simon's luck.

MUNRO, ALICE, 1931-   MsC 37.16.17
    Three parties : short story fragment, n.d.

    1 item : 7 p.
    Typescript. Untitled. Related to material titled
    Three parties in preceding files. Sections similar to
    Simon's luck.

MUNRO, ALICE, 1931-   MsC 37.16.18
    To the fallen heroes : short story fragments, n.d.

    5 items : 7 p. on 6 leaves.
    Holograph, typescript and typescript with holograph
    revisions. Fragments 1 and 2 titled. 2 p.
    holograph, 5 p. typescript.

MUNRO, ALICE, 1931-   MsC 37.16.19
    To the fallen heroes : short story fragments, n.d.

    3 items : 10 p.
    Typescript. Untitled fragments related to material
    titled To the fallen heroes in the preceding file
    (MsC 37.16.18).

MUNRO, ALICE, 1931–   MsC 37.16.20
    To the fallen heroes : short story fragments, n.d.

    2 items : 5 p.
    Typescript. First fragment titled.

MUNRO, ALICE, 1931–   MsC 37.16.21
    To the fallen heroes : short story fragment, n.d.

    1 item : 4 p.
    Typescript. Opening section similar to part of
    chapter Age of Faith in Lives of girls and women.

MUNRO, ALICE, 1931–   MsC 37.16.22
    To the fallen heroes : short story fragment, n.d.

    3 items : 4 p.
    Typescript. First fragment titled.

MUNRO, ALICE, 1931–   MsC 37.16.23
    The unfortunate lady : short story fragment, 1951.

    1 item : 10 p.
    Typescript. Signed "Alice Laidlaw (Mrs. J.
    Munro)". Date written established as Summer 1951
    by A. Munro.

MUNRO, ALICE, 1931–   MsC 37.16.24
    Upward mobility : short story fragments, n.d.

    2 items : 2 p.
    Holograph and typescript. Holograph title on both
    fragments.

MUNRO, ALICE, 1931–   MsC 37.16.25
    Waiting : short story fragment, n.d.

    1 item : 4 p.
    Typescript.

MUNRO, ALICE, 1931–   MsC 37.16.26
    The war hero, the boy murderer, the lady
    ventriloquist : short story fragments, n.d.

    2 items : 5 p.
    Holograph. Untitled fragments similar to material
    titled The war hero, the boy murderer, the lady
    ventriloquist in the following file. Fragments
    possibly from same draft. For related material see
    also The boy murderer.

MUNRO, ALICE, 1931–   MsC 37.16.27
    The war hero, the boy murderer, the lady
    ventriloquist : short story fragments, n.d.

    1 item : 9 p.
    Typescript with holograph corrections. Related
    material titled The boy murderer.

MUNRO, ALICE, 1931–   MsC 37.16.28
    The war hero, the boy murderer, the lady
    ventriloquist : short story fragments, n.d.

    21 items : 51 p. on 50 leaves.
    Holograph, typescript and typescript with holograph
    revisions. Untitled fragments about "Franklin"
    coming home from the war. Related material titled
    The war hero, the boy murderer, the lady
    ventriloquist in preceding files. For related material
    see also The boy murderer. 1 p. holograph, 50 p.
    typescript.

MUNRO, ALICE, 1931–   MsC 37.16.29
  The war hero, the boy murderer, the lady
  ventriloquist : short story fragments, n.d.

    4 items : 25 p.
    Typescript and typescript with holograph revisions.
    Untitled fragments about "Franklin" coming home
    from the war. Similar to material titled The war
    hero, the boy murderer, the lady ventriloquist in
    preceding files. For related material see also The
    boy murderer. Items 2–4 have sections related to
    chapters titled Lives of girls and women and
    Princess Ida in novel Lives of girls and women. One
    page insert with holograph annotation "one sheet" in
    item 4.

MUNRO, ALICE, 1931–   MsC 37.16.30
  The war hero, the boy murderer, the lady
  ventriloquist : short story fragments, n.d.

    5 items : 6 p.
    Typescript. Untitled miscellaneous fragments related
    to material titled The war hero, the boy murderer,
    the lady ventriloquist and The boy murderer.

MUNRO, ALICE, 1931–   MsC 37.16.31
  Watering : short story(?) fragment, n.d.

    1 item : 1 p.
    Typescript. Short descriptive work about watering
    the garden.

MUNRO, ALICE, 1931–   MsC 37.16.32
  Weekend : short story fragments, n.d.

    15 items : 31 p. on 27 leaves.
    Holograph and typescript. Second item titled.
    Short story fragments about going to London, Ont.
    to find a summer job. 8 p. holograph, 23 p.
    typescript.

MUNRO, ALICE, 1931–   MsC 37.16.33
    The white kitten : short story fragments, n.d.

    2 items : 2 p.
    Typescript. First fragment titled.

MUNRO, ALICE, 1931–   MsC 37.16.34
    The yellow afternoon : short story fragment, 1951.

    1 item : 11 p.
    Typescript (carbon copy) with holograph revisions.
    Includes p. 1-10, 12. Date written established as
    Summer 1951 by A. Munro.

MUNRO, ALICE, 1931-   MsC 37.16.35-
NOTEBOOK AND UNTITLED FRAGMENT SERIES,   37.19.71
CA. 1950-1978.

483 ITEMS.
CONSISTS OF NOTEBOOKS AND UNTITLED FRAGMENTS
WHICH COULD NOT BE CLOSELY RELATED TO TITLED
MATERIAL. NOTEBOOKS CONTAIN HOLOGRAPH
FRAGMENTS, MOST PRELIMINARY WORK FOR SHORT
STORIES OR NOVEL LIVES OF GIRLS AND WOMEN;
DATED BY A. MUNRO AND ARRANGED
CHRONOLOGICALLY. NOTEBOOKS FOLLOWED BY
UNDATED, UNTITLED FRAGMENTS SORTED INTO TWO
GROUPS: THOSE BELIEVED WRITTEN BEFORE 1970,
MOST SET IN RURAL ONTARIO; AND THOSE BELIEVED
WRITTEN IN THE LATE 1960s OR THE 1970s, MOST SET
IN URBAN CENTRES OR INVOLVING A RETURN TO
HOMETOWNS IN ONTARIO. SOME OVERLAP OCCURS
BETWEEN GROUPS. FRAGMENTS DESCRIBED ONLY IF
RELATED TO TITLED WORKS OR IF WARRANTED BY A
SUBSTANTIAL AMOUNT OF SIMILAR MATERIAL. IN
EACH TENTATIVELY DATED FRAGMENT SECTION,
DESCRIBED MATERIAL IS FOLLOWED BY
MISCELLANEOUS FRAGMENTS.

MUNRO, ALICE, 1931-   MsC 37.16.35
    Notebook, 196-.

    1 item : 29 p. on 18 leaves.
    Orange notebook with holograph text. Includes
    17 p. poetry, ten untitled fragments and one
    fragment titled Rapunzel, Rapunzel. Most poems
    untitled; one poem titled Lower Wingham, 1938 and
    another related to short story Images. A. Munro
    established date as 1960s and advised that fragments
    relate to early Lives of girls and women material.

MUNRO, ALICE, 1931-   MsC 37.16.36
    Notebook, 196-.

    1 item : 10 p. on 6 leaves.
    Yellow notebook with holograph text. Includes five
    untitled fragments, some related to chapters Age of
    faith and Changes and ceremonies in novel Lives of
    girls and women and to short story fragments titled
    I am the daughter of a river god. Date established
    by A. Munro. Second half of notebook contains
    sketches of faces.

MUNRO, ALICE, 1931–   MsC 37.16.37
   Notebook, 196–.

1 item : 23 p. on 22 leaves.
Brown coil notebook with holograph text. One
holograph map, eight untitled fragments, three
fragments titled Burglars, Show me your arm and
Three women. Most fragments are early drafts of
material in novel Lives of girls and women,
particularly chapters Age of faith, Changes and
ceremonies, Epilogue : the photographer, The Flats
Road, Heirs of the living body and Lives of girls
and women. Page 1 contains holograph map,
probably of Jubilee. Also includes text for Author's
commentary, A. Munro's interpretation of Boys and
girls, published in Sixteen by twelve : short stories
by Canadian writers/edited by John Metcalf, 1970;
and a short note about writing An ounce of cure.
Date identified as 1960s by A. Munro.

MUNRO, ALICE, 1931–   MsC 37.16.38
   Notebook, 197–.

1 item : 24 p.
Red coil notebook with holograph text. Includes two
story outlines, eight untitled fragments and one
fragment titled Dr. Needle. Untitled fragments
related to early drafts of Half a grapefruit,
Characters and photo album text. Contents indicate
notebook belongs with those dated as written after
1974 by A. Munro.

MUNRO, ALICE, 1931–   MsC 37.16.39
   Notebook, 197–.

1 item : 12 p.
White and green writing pad with holograph text.
Includes six untitled fragments. Fragments 3 and 4
related to Simon's luck and Royal beatings
respectively. Last two fragments in different
handwriting, not certain if written by A. Munro.
Contents indicate notebook belongs with those dated
as written after 1974 by A. Munro.

MUNRO, ALICE, 1931–   MsC 37.17.1
    Notebook, 197-.

    1 item : 8 p.
    Lined notepad with holograph text. Includes story
    outline and three untitled fragments, the last related
    to Providence. Material generally related to early
    drafts of short stories in Who do you think you are?
    and so indicate that notebook belongs with those
    dated as written after 1974 by A. Munro.

MUNRO, ALICE, 1931–   MsC 37.17.2
    Notebook, 197-.

    1 item : 33 p. on 32 leaves.
    Coil notebook with photograph of girl on cover.
    Holograph text. Includes three outlines, one for
    The beggar maid and two possibly related to early
    work on short story collection Who do you think you
    are?. Also includes fourteen untitled fragments and
    six fragments titled Cement block house, Natural
    mistakes, Butcher's meat, Silver wedding, Dr.
    Needle's daughter and Suicide ladies. Several
    fragments relate to stories in Who do you think you
    are?, particularly Royal beatings, The beggar maid
    and Spelling, and to fragments titled Dr. Needle.
    Five fragments, including one titled Natural
    mistakes, are about teaching creative writing at a
    mountain university. Date established as after 1974
    by A. Munro.

MUNRO, ALICE, 1931–   MsC 37.17.3
    Notebook, 197-.

    1 item : 13 p.
    White and green writing pad with holograph text.
    Includes five untitled fragments and one fragment
    titled Suicide ladies. Verso of front cover has list
    of numbers; rear cover has list of short story titles,
    most of which were published in collections Who do
    you think you are? or The moons of Jupiter. Date
    established as after 1974 by A. Munro.

MUNRO, ALICE, 1931–   MsC 37.17.4
    Notebook, 197–.

    1 item : 7 p.
    Grey notebook with holograph text. Contains six
    untitled fragments, several similar to material titled
    Suicide ladies. Date established as after 1974 by
    A. Munro.

MUNRO, ALICE, 1931–   MsC 37.17.5
    Notebook, 197–.

    1 item : 6 p.
    Grey notebook with holograph text. Contains two
    untitled fragments, one fragment titled Simon's luck
    and two outlines, one related to short story
    collection Who do you think you are?, the other
    unidentified. Fragments related to, or extensions
    of, "Rose" stories in Who do you think you are?.
    Date established as after 1974 by A. Munro.

MUNRO, ALICE, 1931–   MsC 37.17.6
    Notebook, 197–.

    1 item : 21 p. on 19 leaves.
    Blue notebook with holograph text. Incudes nine
    untitled fragments, four related to Mischief; two
    fragments titled Simon (similar to sections of Simon's
    luck) and Old Mr. Black; two outlines, one for
    Mischief, the other possibly related to Simon and
    Elaine, Simon's luck and/or Mischief. Date
    established as after 1974 by A. Munro.

MUNRO, ALICE, 1931–   MsC 37.17.7
    Notebook, 197–.

    1 item : 2 p.
    Yellow notebook with holograph text. Contains
    fragment titled Suicide ladies. Date established as
    after 1974 by A. Munro.

MUNRO, ALICE, 1931–   MsC 37.17.8
     Untitled fragment, 196–(?).

     1 item : 2 p.
     Typescript. Section similar to description of
     children's bedroom in Boys and girls.

MUNRO, ALICE, 1931–   MsC 37.17.9
     Untitled fragment, 196–(?).

     1 item : 1 p.
     Holograph. Section similar to Images.

MUNRO, ALICE, 1931–   MsC 37.17.10
     Untitled fragments, 196–(?).

     2 items : 2 p.
     Typescript. Beginning paragraph similar to A trip
     to the coast.

MUNRO, ALICE, 1931–   MsC 37.17.11
     Untitled fragment, 196–(?).

     1 item : 1 p.
     Typescript. Beginning section similar to How I met
     my husband.

MUNRO, ALICE, 1931–   MsC 37.17.12
     Untitled fragment, 196–(?).

     1 item : 1 p.
     Typescript. Section similar to How I met my
     husband.

MUNRO, ALICE, 1931–   MsC 37.17.13-21
    Untitled fragments, 196–(?).

    39 items : 120 p. on 116 leaves.
    Holograph, typescript and typescript with holograph
    revisions. Untitled fragments about a girl and her
    grandmother, usually called Mrs. Jordan. Many
    fragments are set in Jubilee and are probably
    preliminary work for novel Lives of girls and women.
    Some fragments relate particularly to chapters Age of
    faith, Baptizing, Changes and ceremonies and
    Princess Ida. Similar fragments, possibly from same
    draft, have been filed together with exception of
    MsC 37.17.21, which contains miscellaneous
    fragments. 2 p. holograph, 117 p. typescript.

MUNRO, ALICE, 1931–   MsC 37.17.22-42
    Untitled fragments, 196–(?).

    54 items : 134 p. on 133 leaves.
    Holograph, typescript and typescript with holograph
    additions and revisions. Untitled fragments about
    the Jordans and McKays. Most fragments set in
    Jubilee, particularly describing life on Flats Road.
    Several fragments in MsC 37.17.30-40 describe a
    plane landing in Jubilee. Much of the material is
    probably preliminary work for novel Lives of girls
    and women; MsC 37.17.23 is also related to
    fragments titled The boy murderer. Similar
    fragments filed together with exception of
    MsC 37.17.42, which contains miscellaneous
    fragments. MsC 37.17.27 included because of
    similarity to preceding file. 10 p. holograph, 124 p.
    typescript.

MUNRO, ALICE, 1931–   MsC 37.17.43-44
    Untitled fragments, 196–(?).

    14 items : 22 p.
    Typescript. Fragments about various girls at a
    United Church summer camp. For other possibly
    related "Naomi" material see following file and
    fragments titled Weekend.

MUNRO, ALICE, 1931–   MsC 37.17.45
    Untitled fragments, 196-(?).

    12 items : 46 p.
    Holograph, typescript and typescript with holograph
    revisions. Fragments about high school friendship
    with a girl, usually called Naomi Ferguson. Material
    possibly preliminary work for novel Lives of girls
    and women, particularly chapter Lives of girls and
    women. For other "Naomi" material, see preceding
    file and fragments titled Weekend.

MUNRO, ALICE, 1931–   MsC 37.18.1
    Untitled fragments, 196-(?).

    15 items : 17 p.
    Typescript and typescript with holograph revisions.
    Fragments about high school relationships, possibly
    preliminary work for novel Lives of girls and women.
    Some sections related particularly to chapters
    Changes and ceremonies and Lives of girls and
    women, and one section to short story The found
    boat.

MUNRO, ALICE, 1931–   MsC 37.18.2
    Untitled fragments, 196-(?).

    2 items : 6 p.
    Typescript and typescript with holograph revisions.
    Fragments with sections rewritten and included in
    chapter Lives of girls and women in novel of the
    same name.

MUNRO, ALICE, 1931–   MsC 37.18.3
    Untitled fragments, 196-(?).

    6 items : 22 p.
    Typescript and typescript with holograph revisions.
    Fragments set in Jubilee about the Holloway family.
    Sections in the last two fragments about evangelical
    meeting promotion, similar to parts of chapter
    Baptizing in novel Lives of girls and women.

MUNRO, ALICE, 1931–   MsC 37.18.4
    Untitled fragments, 196-(?).

    6 items : 8 p.
    Holograph and typescript. Set in Jubilee; most
    fragments begin with parents napping after dinner.
    Holograph fragment has burglar section similar to
    beginning of chapter Age of faith in novel Lives of
    girls and women. 3 p. holograph, 5 p. typescript.

MUNRO, ALICE, 1931–   MsC 37.18.5
    Untitled fragment, 196-(?).

    1 item : 5 p. on 4 leaves.
    Typescript with holograph revisions. Section about
    mother having Parkinson's disease. Possibly
    preliminary work for novel Lives of girls and women,
    particularly chapter Princess Ida. Unrelated text on
    verso of last page.

MUNRO, ALICE, 1931–   MsC 37.18.6
    Untitled fragments, 196-(?).

    5 items : 7 p. on 5 leaves.
    Holograph and typescript. Fragments beginning "My
    mother had Parkinson's disease". Holograph text in
    unidentified handwriting on verso of first item.
    Verso of item 2 has poetry fragments.

MUNRO, ALICE, 1931–   MsC 37.18.7
    Untitled fragments, 196-(?).

    3 items : 21 p.
    Typescript. Fragments beginning "Agnes Jardine
    sat on her screened porch...". Set in Wawanash,
    about Jardine family and their neighbours.

MUNRO, ALICE, 1931–   MsC 37.18.8
    Untitled fragments, 196-(?).

        15 items : 23 p. on 22 leaves.
        Typescript. Fragments all beginning with various
        women attending a Great Books discussion group.

MUNRO, ALICE, 1931–   MsC 37.18.9-11
    Untitled fragments, 196-(?).

        12 items : 15 p. on 14 leaves.
        Typescript fragments describing Jubilee and
        Wawanash.

MUNRO, ALICE, 1931–   MsC 37.18.12
    Untitled fragment, not after 1970.

        1 item : 1 p.
        Holograph list of unidentified titles.

MUNRO, ALICE, 1931–   MsC 37.18.13-20
    Untitled fragments, not after 1970.

        20 items : 28 p. on 25 leaves.
        Holograph and typescript. Miscellaneous holograph
        fragments, most set in rural Ontario. 20 p.
        holograph, 8 p. typescript.

MUNRO, ALICE, 1931–   MsC 37.18.21-
    Untitled fragments, not after 1970.   37.19.16

        127 items : 234 p. on 215 leaves.
        Typescript and typescript with holograph revisions.
        Miscellaneous fragments, probably written before
        1970; most set in small towns in rural Ontario. Some
        fragments may be preliminary work for short stories
        in Dance of the happy shades or for novel Lives of
        girls and women. Fragments of less than one page
        are filed in MsC 37.19.16.

MUNRO, ALICE, 1931–   MsC 37.19.17
Untitled fragments, 197–(?).

3 items : 4 p.
Typescript and typescript with holograph revision.
Fragments about a woman attempting suicide.   Similar
material, titled Suicide ladies, in notebook
MsC 37.17.2.

MUNRO, ALICE, 1931–   MsC 37.19.18
Untitled fragment, 197–(?).

1 item : 4 p.
Typescript.   Fragment with sections similar to parts
of The beggar maid.

MUNRO, ALICE, 1931–   MsC 37.19.19
Untitled fragments, 197–(?).

4 items : 12 p.
Typescript and typescript with holograph deletion.
Fragments with sections similar to parts of Mischief.
First two items may be consecutive.

MUNRO, ALICE, 1931–   MsC 37.19.20
Untitled fragments, 197–(?).

5 items : 18 p.
Typescript and typescript with holograph revisions.
Fragments which begin with various married couples
shopping for garden ornaments.   Possibly
preliminary work for Mischief.   Last two items may
be from same draft.

MUNRO, ALICE, 1931–   MsC 37.19.21
Untitled fragment, 197–(?).

1 item : 1 p.
Typescript.   Fragment with some similarity to Royal
beatings.

MUNRO, ALICE, 1931–   MsC 37.19.22
    Untitled fragments, 197–(?).

    2 items : 7 p. on 6 leaves.
    Typescript with holograph text on verso of last
    page. Fragments about a lover, Gabriel or Simon.
    Sections similar to Sheila version of Simon's luck.
    Items possibly from one draft, although the lover's
    name changes.

MUNRO, ALICE, 1931–   MsC 37.19.23
    Untitled fragments, 197–(?).

    9 items : 34 p.
    Typescript and typescript with holograph revisions.
    Untitled fragments with segments related to, or
    extensions of, various stories in Who do you think
    you are?, especially The beggar maid, Mischief,
    Providence and Simon's luck. Last fragment also has
    section related to Chaddeleys and Flemings.

MUNRO, ALICE, 1931–   MsC 37.19.24
    Untitled fragment, 197–(?).

    1 item : 1 p.
    Typescript. Untitled fragment related to stories in
    collection Who do you think you are?.

MUNRO, ALICE, 1931–   MsC 37.19.25
    Untitled fragment, 197–(?).

    1 item : 2 p.
    Typescript. Untitled fragment related to stories in
    collection Who do you think you are?.

MUNRO, ALICE, 1931–   MsC 37.19.26
    Untitled fragments, 197–(?).

    11 items : 28 p. on 27 leaves.
    Holograph, typescript and typescript with holograph
    revisions. Fragments beginning with a woman,
    usually called Frances, believing the man at the door
    is a blackmailer. Similar material, titled Dr. Needle,
    in notebook MsC 37.16.38. Short typescript
    fragment, titled Dr. Neeley's daughter, on verso of
    last page of item 5. 3 p. holograph, 25 p.
    typescript.

MUNRO, ALICE, 1931–   MsC 37.19.27
    Untitled fragments, 197–(?).

    12 items : 29 p.
    Holograph, typescript and typescript with holograph
    revisions. Short story fragments about teaching
    creative writing at university in the Kootenay
    mountains. (For similar material see fragments, one
    titled Natural mistakes, in notebook MsC 37.17.2.)
    Several versions included. Verso of first page
    contains list of stories. 4 p. holograph, 25 p.
    typescript.

MUNRO, ALICE, 1931–   MsC 37.19.28-29
    Untitled fragments, 197–(?).

    13 items : 44 p.
    Typescript and typescript with holograph revisions.
    Fragments about two young married couples, usually
    called Bob and Emily and Frank and Norah, living in
    suburbs of Vancouver.

MUNRO, ALICE, 1931–   MsC 37.19.30-71
    Untitled fragments, between 1960 and 1978.

    70 items : 123 p.
    Holograph, typescript and typescript with holograph
    revisions. Miscellaneous fragments probably written
    between the late 1960s and 1978. Most fragments are
    set in urban centres, many in B.C., or involve
    return to home towns in rural Ontario. Some
    fragments may be preliminary work for short stories
    in collections Something I've been meaning to tell you
    and Who do you think you are?. Fragments of less
    than one-half page are filed in MsC 37.19.71. 2 p.
    holograph, 121 p. typescript.

MUNRO, ALICE, 1931–   MsC 37.20.1-12
TELEVISION SERIES, CA. 1976-1978.

17 ITEMS.
CONSISTS OF PRELIMINARY WORK AND SCRIPTS FOR
SCREENPLAY 1847 : THE IRISH, PART OF THE
TELEVISION SERIES THE NEWCOMERS/LES ARRIVANTS;
AND MANUSCRIPTS FOR PRINT ADAPTATION OF THIS
SCREENPLAY, TITLED A BETTER PLACE THAN HOME,
PUBLISHED IN THE NEWCOMERS : INHABITING A NEW
LAND. FILES ARRANGED CHRONOLOGICALLY.

MUNRO, ALICE, 1931–   MsC 37.20.1
     1847 : the Irish : preliminary notes, n.d.

     1 item : 1 p.
     Holograph. Two textual fragments used in later
     drafts of 1847 : the Irish, part of the television
     series The newcomers/Les arrivants.

MUNRO, ALICE, 1931–   MsC 37.20.2
     1847 : the Irish : preliminary script, n.d.

     2 items : 13 p.
     Holograph "treatment possibility". Untitled. Later
     titled 1847 : the Irish; first telecast on
     January 8, 1978, by Canadian Broadcasting
     Corporation, as part of the series The
     newcomers/Les arrivants.

MUNRO, ALICE, 1931–   MsC 37.20.3
     1847 : the Irish : preliminary script, n.d.

     3 items : 18 p.
     Typescript with holograph notes, additions and
     revisions. Untitled. Includes "treatment
     possibility", 16 p.; and two pages of "Notes on this
     treatment" with page missing. Later titled
     1847 : the Irish, part of Canadian Broadcasting
     Corporation television series The newcomers/Les
     arrivants.

MUNRO, ALICE, 1931–   MsC 37.20.4
    1847 : the Irish : television script, n.d.

    2 items : 17 p.
    Typescript (photocopy). Includes untitled script
    and two pages of "Notes on treatment". Later titled
    1847 : the Irish, part of the Canadian Broadcasting
    Corporation television series The newscomers/Les
    arrivants.

MUNRO, ALICE, 1931–   MsC 37.20.5
    1847 : the Irish : television script fragment, n.d.

    1 item : 28 p.
    Typescript. Untitled script with ending missing.
    Later titled 1847 : the Irish, part of Canadian
    Broadcasting Corporation television series The
    newscomers/Les arrivants.

MUNRO, ALICE, 1931–   MsC 37.20.6
    1847 : the Irish : television script fragments, n.d.

    2 items : 6 p.
    Typescript (photocopy). Photocopied from script in
    preceding file. Untitled fragments from television
    script later titled 1847 : the Irish, part of Canadian
    Broadcasting Corporation series The newscomers/Les
    arrivants.

MUNRO, ALICE, 1931–   MsC 37.20.7
    1847 : the Irish : television script, n.d.

    1 item : 45 p.
    Typescript with holograph revisions (photocopy).
    Untitled script, later titled 1847 : the Irish, part of
    Canadian Broadcasting Corporation television series
    The newscomers/Les arrivants.

MUNRO, ALICE, 1931-   MsC 37.20.8
1847 : the Irish : revised draft, n.d.

1 item : 66 p.
Typescript (photocopy). Title page reads
"UNTITLED IRISH SCRIPT by Alice Munro
REVISED DRAFT". Later titled 1847 : the Irish,
part of Canadian Broadcasting Corporation television
series The newcomers/Les arrivants.

MUNRO, ALICE, 1931-   MsC 37.20.9
1847 : the Irish : revised shooting script, 1976(?).

1 item : 53 p.
Typescript (photocopy). Untitled script, later titled
1847 : the Irish, part of the Canadian Broadcasting
Corporation television series The newcomers/Les
arrivants, commissioned by Imperial Oil Limited to
celebrate its 100th anniversary. Includes repository
photocopy of covering letter (original in
MsC 37.2.31) dated January 4, 1977, from Nielsen-
Ferns Inc., producers of the series, explaining
revisions made to the script.

MUNRO, ALICE, 1931-   MsC 37.20.10
A better place than home : short story fragment,
n.d.

1 item : 4 p. on 3 leaves.
Typescript with one holograph revision. Fragment
from unidentified draft of A better place than home,
the print adaptation of 1847 : the Irish. Published
in The newcomers : inhabiting a new land. (General
editor Charles E. Israel. Toronto: McClelland and
Stewart, 1979.) Holograph annotation on last page.

MUNRO, ALICE, 1931-   MsC 37.20.11
A better place than home : short story fragment,
n.d.

1 item : 19 p.
Typescript with holograph revisions. Untitled,
incomplete draft of A better place than home, the
print adaptation of 1847 : the Irish. Published in
the newcomers : inhabiting a new land. (Edited by
Charles E. Israel. Toronto: McClelland and
Stewart, 1979.)

MUNRO, ALICE, 1931–   MsC 37.20.12
    1847 : short story, n.d.

    1 item : 19 p.
    Typescript with holograph revisions, title and
    pagination.   Titled 1847, later published as A better
    place than home in The newcomers : inhabiting a
    new land.   (Edited by Charles E. Israel.   Toronto:
    McClelland and Stewart, 1979.)   Story version of
    television screenplay 1847 : the Irish.

MUNRO, ALICE, 1931–   MsC 37.20.13
POETRY SERIES, N.D.

21 ITEMS.
CONSISTS OF ONE FILE (35 P. ON 31 LEAVES;
TYPESCRIPT AND HOLOGRAPH) CONTAINING ELEVEN
UNTITLED POEMS. SOME POEMS HAVE MORE THAN ONE
DRAFT. ONE POEM, ITEM 18, POSSIBLY RELATED TO
SHORT STORY IMAGES. TITLE PAGE AND SEVERAL
POEMS SIGNED ANNE CHAMNEY, PSEUDONYM OF
A. MUNRO. FOR EARLY DRAFTS OF MANY OF THESE
POEMS SEE NOTEBOOK MSC 37.16.35.

MUNRO, ALICE, 1931-   MsC 37.20.14-18
NON-FICTION SERIES, CA. 1962-1978.

5 ITEMS.
CONSISTS OF ARTICLE EVERYTHING HERE IS
TOUCHABLE AND MYSTERIOUS AND ESSAYS REMEMBER
ROGER MORTIMER?, THE COLONEL'S HASH RESETTLED
AND ON WRITING "THE OFFICE". FILES ARRANGED
CHRONOLOGICALLY.

MUNRO, ALICE, 1931-   MsC 37.20.14
    Remember Roger Mortimer? : essay fragment, n.d.

    1 item : 10 p.
    Typescript. Incomplete. Published as Remember
    Roger Mortimer : Dickens' "Child's history of
    England" remembered in the Montrealer, v. 36,
    no. 2, February 1962.

MUNRO, ALICE, 1931-   MsC 37.20.15
    The colonel's hash resettled : author's commentary,
    n.d.

    1 item : 3 p.
    Typescript with holograph additions and revisions.
    Untitled; title later assigned by John Metcalf.
    A. Munro's commentary on short stories Images and
    Dance of the happy shades. These stories and the
    commentary published in The narrative voice : short
    stories and reflections by Canadian authors. (Edited
    by John Metcalf. Toronto: McGraw-Hill Ryerson,
    1972.)

MUNRO, ALICE, 1931-   MsC 37.20.16
    Everything here is touchable and
    mysterious : article, n.d.

    1 item : 2 p.
    Typescript with holograph revisions (photocopy).
    Untitled. Descriptive article about Wingham, Ont.,
    published as Everything here is touchable and
    mysterious. (See following file MsC 37.20.17.)

MUNRO, ALICE, 1931-   MsC 37.20.17
    Everything here is touchable and
    mysterious : article.

    1 item : 1 p.
    Photocopy of article published in Weekend Magazine,
    v. 24, no. 19, May 11, 1974. Information at top of
    page showing title as Something I've been meaning to
    tell you is incorrect.

MUNRO, ALICE, 1931-   MsC 37.20.18
    On writing "The office" : author's commentary,
    1978(?).

    1 item : 2 p.
    Possibly author's page proofs for A. Munro's
    commentary on short story The office, published in
    Transitions II : short fiction : a source book of
    Canadian literature. (Edited by Edward Peck.
    Vancouver: Commcept Publishing Ltd., 1978.)
    Holograph annotation "copy 1" on title page.

MUNRO, ALICE, 1931–   MsC 37.20.19-26
WORKS ON ALICE MUNRO SERIES, 1957-1979.

38 ITEMS.
CONSISTS OF INTERVIEWS WITH, AND ARTICLES ON,
A. MUNRO, FOLLOWED BY THREE ESSAYS AND A
SPEECH ON A. MUNRO'S FICTION. INTERVIEWS
ARRANGED CHRONOLOGICALLY, FOLLOWED BY ONE
FILE OF NEWSPAPER ARTICLES, ALSO ARRANGED
CHRONOLOGICALLY. ESSAYS AND SPEECH ON
A. MUNRO'S WORK FILED ALPHABETICALLY BY
AUTHOR.

FRUM, BARBARA.   MsC 37.20.19
    Great dames.
    p. 32-38, 68.

    In Maclean's, v. 86, no. 4, April 1973. Barbara
    Frum interviews six Canadian women, one of whom is
    Alice Munro.

MARTINEAU, BARBARA.   MsC 37.20.20
    Alice Munro interviewed by Barbara
    Martineau : interview, 1975 February 16.

    1 item : 31 p.
    Typescript with holograph revisions (photocopy).
    Place given as London, Ont. Transcript of a tape
    recorded interview with Alice Munro.

MURCH, KEM.   MsC 37.20.21
    Name – Alice Munro, occupation – writer.
    p. 42-43, 69-72.

    In Chatelaine, v. 48, no. 8, August 1975. Interview
    with Alice Munro. Includes duplicate copy of
    interview, detached from Chatelaine.

MUNRO, ALICE, 1931-
    Newspaper articles about A. Munro and her work,
n.d., 1957 June 28-1979 March 22.

    31 items : 34 p. on 33 leaves.
Newsclippings and photocopies of articles from
various newspapers. Included among various topics
are articles about awards won by A. Munro, such as
the 1968 and 1978 Governor General's Literary
Awards and the 1977 Canada-Australia Literary
Prize.

MsC 37.20.22

DAHLIE, HALLVARD.
    The fiction of Alice Munro : essay, n.d.

    1 item : 21 p.
Typescript (photocopy) draft of essay, later
published in Ploughshares, v. 4, no. 3, 1978.

MsC 37.20.23

DAHLIE, HALLVARD.
    Unconsummated relationships : isolation and rejection
in Alice Munro's stories : essay.
p. 43-48.

    Photocopy of essay from World Literature Written in
English, v. 11, no. 1, April 1972. Holograph
annotation on last page identifies the periodical.

MsC 37.20.24

RUSSELL, BONNIE.
    Alice Munro : a story-maker : essay, n.d.

    1 item : 15 p.
Typescript (photocopy). Student's essay for English
384 at unidentified university. Includes marker's
holograph comments and criticisms.

MsC 37.20.25

TOPPINGS, EARLE.
    Alice Munro : talk to the Women's University Club,
Oshawa, April 13/77 : speech.

    1 item : 22 p.
Typescript (carbon copy). Includes holograph
annotations "May 2/77" and "(by Earle Toppings)".

MsC 37.20.26

MUNRO, ALICE, 1931–   MsC 37.20.27-32
MISCELLANEOUS SERIES, N.D., 1961-1975.

14 ITEMS.
CONSISTS OF SEVERAL SHORT STORY MANUSCRIPTS
AND FRAGMENTS WRITTEN BY AUTHORS OTHER THAN
A. MUNRO, ARRANGED ALPHABETICALLY BY AUTHOR,
AND ONE FILE OF MISCELLANEOUS NEWSPAPER AND
JOURNAL CLIPPINGS.

Good night, Jamie : short story, n.d.   MsC 37.20.27

    1 item : 6 p.
    Typescript (mimeograph). Author unidentified.

____, JOHN.   MsC 37.20.28
    Untitled short story fragment, n.d.

    1 item : 2 p.
    Typescript (photocopy). Second page includes
    holograph note, signed "John", asking Alice Munro
    to comment on the story.

GAMMAGE, GEORGE.   MsC 37.20.29
    The guide : short story fragment, n.d.

    1 item : 3 p.
    Typescript with holograph corrections.

LAIDLAW, ROBERT E.   MsC 37.20.30
    A day and a half : short story, n.d.

    1 item : 27 p.
    Typescript with holograph corrections and margin
    annotations. Identified by Alice Munro as having
    been written by her father, R. E. Laidlaw.

MUNRO, JAMES.   MsC 37.20.31
    The sanitary engineer : short story fragment, n.d.

    1 item : 3 p.
    Typescript. Identified by Alice Munro as having
    been written by J. Munro.

MUNRO, ALICE, 1931-   MsC 37.20.32
    Miscellaneous clippings, n.d.,
    1961 February-1974 April 30.

    9 items : 21 p. on 15 leaves.
    Miscellaneous clippings and photocopies of articles
    and poems from various newspapers and periodicals,
    none directly related to A. Munro.

Indexes

Alphabetical Listing of Alice Munro's Titles

1847, 37.20.12
1847 : the Irish
    37.2.31
    37.20.1-12
Accident
    37.2.20.7
    37.2.40.1
    37.2.47.4
    37.2.47.12
    37.2.47.18
    37.13.15-28
Age of faith
    37.3.12-14
    37.16.21
    37.16.36-37
    37.17.13-21
    37.18.4
Ambassador from Marrakesh, 37.8.5-6
Ancestors, 37.14.3
Angela, 37.11.26
Angie, 37.14.15
Another life, 37.14.16
The art of fiction, 37.14.17
At the other place, 37.14.18
Author's commentary, 37.16.37
Baptizing
    37.2.25.6
    37.4.1-7
    37.17.13-21
    37.18.3
A basket of strawberries, 37.14.19
The beggar maid
    37.2.18
    37.2.20.7
    37.2.30.2-4
    37.2.47.4
    37.2.47.13-15
    37.2.47.18
    37.2.55.15-19
    37.2.55.21
    37.6.51
    37.9.5-17
    37.12.12
    37.17.2
    37.19.18
    37.19.23
A better place than home
    37.2.22.3
    37.2.47.20
    37.20.10-12
The boy murderer
    37.14.20-26
    37.15.3
    37.16.26-30
    37.17.23

Index